Healing Simplified:
How to Access Your Personal Codes to Transformation

Tonya Cox Turrell

and Carolanne Anselmo

For permission requests, email the publisher or author at
tonyacturrell@gmail.com.

To contact the publisher or author, visit www.tonyaturrell.com or
www.healingsimplified.com

To contact Carolanne Anselmo, visit
www.healingenergyandlearning.com or email
healingenergyandlearning@gmail.com

ISBN-13: 978-1511413336
ISBN-10: 1511413336

Cover photography © by Britt Pavelchak
Graphic design by Marc Mitchell and Jack Schlifer
Edited by Allison M. Schultz

HEAL Technique® is a registered trademark owned by Healing Energy
and Learning – HEAL, LLC.

Our intention for this book:

That you remember the truth of who you are and claim the power that is your birthright,

That you shift out of your head and into your heart,

That you reclaim all of the energy that you've given away to programs and belief systems that have not served your highest good,

That you experience your life from the highest vibration possible,

That we reach a critical mass in a shift to a new state of consciousness, and

That one of you is the hundredth monkey!

This is a book about healing and transformation, but the irony is that you don't need it. You are not broken. You don't need to be healed. You might just need a reminder of the power within you. A nudge. Or a kick in the ass. Let this book be that for you.

NOTE FROM THE AUTHORS

When Carolanne and I started thinking about this book, as we started creating the outline and discussing the message we wanted to convey, I awoke one morning filled with a profound message. From you. *ALL OF YOU.*

I know, it sounds crazy. But hear me out.

One morning not too long ago, I was at the edges of the end of a dream, transitioning from an unconscious to a conscious state. I was in that beautiful ethereal in-between. Not quite asleep, not quite awake. Not fully conscious... but, paradoxically, more conscious than I am in my waking life. And there she was in front of me– my higher self.

Let me stop and explain what I mean by "higher self." This is not a better self or a holier self. What I am talking about here is your all-knowing, unlimited soul. This is an all-knowing, unlimited being of love; the aspect of you that existed before this incarnation and will continue to exist after you shed your physical body; the aspect of you who consciously chose to come down in density to experience feeling and physicality– to know yourself through experience.

As much as we tend to put our higher self on a pedestal, we must realize that our higher selves are as enamored with the physical self as we are of it. We get to feel the summer breeze blowing through our hair, the tender caress of a lover, the enveloping warmth of the sun beating down on our skin, the taste of a sweet, juicy ripe strawberry, the delicious comfort of a chewy-gooey brownie, the melt-your-heart feeling of a child's tiny hand in yours... We are here to experience all these things and more. We are here to create and choose our experiences; to create a life that is art; to know ourselves as artists and creators. We are here to know ourselves as divine, all-knowing, and unlimited beings of love, through experience and, of course, with love.

So, getting back to that encounter with my higher self in the early morning darkness... There she was, waiting on the edges of waking up with anticipation and purpose. She was there to provide me with an introduction to all of you, or rather an aspect of you– your higher selves.

I was still sleepy. Half awake, half asleep. My higher self was nudging me awake, streaming information. She transmitted messages that I couldn't quite grab onto because I was still swimming in drowsiness. On this particular morning, she nudged me awake and told me to get a pen. She was insistent.

"Write it down," the hypnotic and velvety voice of my higher self whispered in the crevices of my sleepy mind.

Let me go back to sleep.

"Write it down! Remember it! Put it in the book!" she persisted. It was more than a gentle nudging. It was almost overwhelming.

I had the realization that this message was not meant just for with me. This was for all of you. I also had the odd feeling that this was not just a nudging from my own soul, but a nudging from many souls. *Dare I say... your soul.*

So I woke up and grabbed my journal and pen. Then I became hyper-aware that the energy in the room was different. It was... *full.* It wasn't just my higher self standing there. Behind her stood the souls of many, hundreds of thousands or more, maybe millions. It felt like the excited energy of walking into a crowded stadium, right there in the dark of my quiet bedroom at 5:30 in the morning.

It is no accident that you are reading this book. By now, you have had enough experience to know that there is no such thing as coincidence. As Albert Einstein said, "Coincidence is God's way of remaining anonymous."[i] Besides, if these words were meant just for me, they would have remained in my journal. But the nudging was so persistent and unrelenting that I got up out of my cozy slumber in response to the insistent voice in my head.

This book is based on our experiences, learnings and insights, as well as a channeling of my higher self, Carolanne's higher self... and, as it turns out, the higher selves of all of you. The intention is that you meet your higher self on these pages. In fact, your soul has led you to this book.

I know this because your soul was whispering to me, along with my own, to write this book. I don't say this lightly or pejoratively. This is not metaphorical. You are reading this book because your soul was one of those whispering to me as I wrote. Your soul is what led you to this book, or what led this book to you. Your soul is what led you to this very moment of reading the words on this page right now. Consider it a love note from your higher self. Consider this book a soul space where your higher self can reach out to connect with you, to help you remember who you really are and to reclaim your rightful authentic power.

Your soul would like you to see your journey from the perspective of the higher self: truly expanded awareness. If you step into that perspective for a moment, you will fully and completely realize that your life is art. You are the creator and the artist, and you are the masterpiece. Everything in your life–every person, experience, obstacle and opportunity–is a call to bring you into something greater. This book is a part of you, moving towards something greater. The ultimate truth of that "something greater" is that you were designed and encoded with infinite love. In fact, your power comes from remembering this simple truth. Now is the time to remember that you are encoded with love. Now is the time to consciously create your life and encode all aspects of all of your creations with love. We, along with your higher selves, invite you to do just that, with love. When you do, you will be amazed and will fall in love with yourself.

That's what it's all about, my love.

WHO WE ARE:

Carolanne:

I have known Carolanne for years. I have seen her heal herself, her family, and countless numbers of clients from physical, emotional and spiritual traumas. She beat more than twenty autoimmune diseases and a doctor's death sentence. Through awakening to her own power, she moved from a devastating diagnosis and instruction from her doctor to get her affairs in order and say her good-byes to guiding and facilitating miracle healings. I can't tell you how many terminal patients I've witnessed who come to her as a last resort, only to transmute the energy of disease and heal themselves at the energetic level, which is the level of source for all of us. Miracles can–and should–be everyday occurrences available to everyone, if you so choose. And that is our intention for this book: to take miracles mainstream by bringing you back to the truth of yourselves, and inviting you to step into your own inherent power.

Not too many years ago, Carolanne's diagnoses led her from the Mayo Clinic in Arizona to the University of Florida's Shands Hospital. She endured fourteen surgeries and was on over seventy medications and supplements, all while trying to raise two toddlers. She had had enough. After a fateful surgery when she woke up under anesthesia, she made the critical decision to live. She claimed her power, which set her on a path of awakening. She began to dabble in alternative healing methods. Instead of preparing for her death, Carolanne decided to investigate. She decided to love harder and live life more fully. She took responsibility for her energy in that moment. That's when a miracle happened. She examined old subconscious programs that clogged her energy, then worked on clearing out the gunk.

Since then, Carolanne's entire life changed. She healed herself. Depression and anxiety instantly lifted as she saw the light at the end of the tunnel. Or, more precisely, she saw the light within herself. Within a couple of months, she was off all medications and in full remission. This newly discovered practice of self-healing brought her face to face with her own power, and she took ownership of her energy. Now she is on a mission to help everyone do the same.

Some people mistakenly call her a healer: Energy healer. Mind-body healer. Spiritual healer. Whatever kind of healer you call her, she is not comfortable with the label because she is not the healer. Not in the traditional sense, anyway. This is because she doesn't perform the healings, you do. She doesn't perform miracles, you do. In fact, she is always the first to tell you that what she can do, *you can do*.

As an "energy healer," Carolanne really is a witness to healings, a witness to miracles, and a facilitator, at most. Facilitating a remembrance and reclamation of your authentic power. Again, and at the risk of sounding like a broken record, you are a powerful, magnificent being. You have all the codes to heal and transform yourself. Carolanne's mission is to bring energy healing and self-empowerment to the mainstream. My mission is to help her.

Tonya:

I met Carolanne seven years ago, and she played an instrumental role in my awakening and the process of coming into my own power. I went to her as a client because I felt unfulfilled as an overworked, overstressed entrepreneur mom of two young boys, trying to manage a fledgling high-tech marketing company with my husband. I say fledgling because, although we were making money, this was at an extremely high personal cost. Stress, anxiety and insomnia plagued us both. I was constantly playing mental chess with money and employee problems. Work drama was always draining my energy. On top of all the stress that my business caused, I did not find my work fulfilling.

I longed for more depth and meaning. I yearned to do something more. On the outside, I'm sure it looked like I was leading a successful life. My team generated millions of dollars in revenue for high profile high-tech clients. I may have achieved a high level of success to the untrained eye, but I was struggling to find significance, and more importantly, peace. On the inside, my spirit was dying. My creativity was withering. My life force was fading. I'd go many nights without sleep and felt a restlessness that I could not quite shake. I felt stuck. Our business paid the bills, just barely sometimes. Our expenses were out of control, and my work did not fulfill the deeper yearnings of my soul. There was no joy. Life just wasn't smooth or gratifying, but I knew there had to be a better way. I contacted Carolanne explicitly to get in touch with my deeper truth, so that I could create a plan to fulfill the greater purpose for my life. Whatever that was.

As my consciousness shifted to a higher frequency, so did the consciousness of my business. At first, that meant total upheaval. Out with the old, in with the new. After the market crash in 2008, all of our business lines of credit collapsed without warning. Making payroll became a bi-weekly nightmare. Insomnia and anxiety moved in with me, rude and unwelcome intruders who stalked me relentlessly, day and night. Chest pains and heart palpitations became my husband's interlopers.

At that time, many of our peers and competitors went out of business, but we held on tightly, trying to hold it together, holding our collective breath the entire time. As owners, my husband and I stopped paying ourselves just to be able to keep our team and infrastructure intact, hoping to ride it out.

Just before Christmas of 2010, things really started to heat up. Thinking of this time reminds me of what the first pilot to break the sound barrier,

Chuck Yeager, said, "Just before you break the sound barrier, the cockpit shakes the most."[ii]

Before any significant breakthrough, there is always immense turbulence. Christmas of 2010 was when our cockpit started thrashing like crazy. Just a couple weeks before the holidays we lost our biggest client, a two million dollar marketing contract with a well-known data storage company that represented about ninety percent of our revenue. It was a death sentence. Having drained all of our cash reserves and with no remaining credit, we had no choice but to begin to release our tight hold. We had to let our entire leadership team go, as well as ninety percent of our employees. It was heartbreaking, devastating, demoralizing and overwhelming. Not only had our entire lives collapsed, but we were now the villains, the employers who had terminated their staff right before Christmas. I mean, who does that except for the embodiment of pure evil? We were not evil, we were just out of options. We were shattered, weary, worn out and drained physically, energetically, emotionally, and financially.

We couldn't pay the rent on the 10,000 square foot office space that we had signed the lease on just nine months before, when we were poised for growth. We sent our remaining staff home to set up home offices, hoping we could make a virtual model work. We couldn't pay the mortgage on our home. We were behind on taxes and had more than $150,000 in IRS debt. We couldn't make our car payments. Our credit score took a pounding. We used the very last of our personal life savings to ensure that each employee was paid their final check. There were one too many shameful visits to the grocery store that ended with me leaving my cart full of groceries at the checkout because there was no money in my account to pay for it. We had a garage sale to sell our office furniture and equipment, plus personal treasures that would provide us with some immediate cash, to help us keep our family afloat while we grieved and tried to figure out our next move. Everything we had worked for, achieved and accumulated in the previous eight years was gone in an instant. We were devastated. But we also suddenly felt very free.

We made the tough choice to dissolve our business. With our new understanding of energy, we wanted to release it. We filed for bankruptcy. There were too many contracts that we simply could not keep due to the downfall of our company and the loss of our income. With bankruptcy came the loss of our home (we were a full year behind on mortgage payments) and our cars. Gratefully, my dad brought his old beat-up Ford pickup from his South Carolina farm for us to drive. At that stage, I felt numb. I was only going through the motions of my life, putting one foot in front of the other, just trying to make it from one day to the next.

I had done so much letting go that year, a lot of crying and cleansing. The existence that I had expended all of my life force energy to build lay in shambles at my feet, along with the splintered dreams that my husband and I had dreamt together. I tried to enjoy the exhale, reminding myself that those shambles were once shackles.

I consistently did the HEAL work because I understood that what was going on in my business was energetic at its source, and I wanted to take responsibility for my energy and my outcomes. I was at a point of destiny on my life path. As is the case with many experiences in life, I understood that I was just going to have to go through it no matter what. The energy I chose to bring to the experience was up to me. I could experience it from a low vibration of feeling sorry for myself and acting like a victim, or I could experience it from a high vibration and choose to see the opportunity in the challenge. The HEAL work revealed patterns in my life where I had chosen the lower expression of self-pity and victimhood in the past, and allowed me to clear the pattern in my cellular memory and reprogram myself for a higher expression.

Then, everything changed. I opened up to the possibilities of something more than I had been able to envision with my limited view from that negative frequency. Like magic, when my energy was clear and my thinking shifted, my mind opened to creativity and all kinds of wonderful ideas popped off like inspiration fireworks. Doing this healing work allowed me to gain the highest possible perspective and build new ways of contemplating a new direction. I saw how we could rebuild our business in a meaningful, impactful way that would still give me time to pursue my dream of writing. My husband and I put our heads together, creativity flowed in, and we were able to reinvent the way we did business, making the work easier, more fun, more effective, and tremendously more profitable. We doubled in revenue every year for four years, making our company a very attractive potential purchase for investors. Four years out of bankruptcy, we sold the business for a handsome price. My life opened up to bigger and better things, far more than I had ever expected, and far better than I had ever hoped for.

Using the HEAL Technique® gave me insight into my own subconscious programs and the patterns they created in my life. The HEAL Technique® helped me to unlock my healing codes so I could quickly and easily move through the mess. The total upheaval was brief and relatively painless because I stayed present to what was going on. Working with the HEAL Technique® helped me to stay very conscious of my programming, so I was no longer a victim of subconscious thought patterns.

Doing the HEAL work allowed me to stay present to what was going on with my life and what I was experiencing energetically. I allowed myself to feel the feelings and move through them. I was shedding the energies that weighed me down. I knew I was manifesting exactly what I had intended. At times, I could sense my higher self reaching out to me reassuringly, reminding me that I was on my path.

As I shifted, everything in my life shifted. My marriage was more loving and fulfilling. My friendships and relationships became deeper and more satisfying. My business–and everything it touched–became more enlightened and awake.

So much of my awakening and transformation has been the result of working directly with the HEAL Technique®. When I look around at my life now, I know I am living in my truth. I know I can be a masterful manifester. I know I am a powerful being. Using the HEAL Technique® taught me that I have all the codes to understanding the truth of who I am and why I am here. My personal journey of transformation has given me a whole new life. In the past, I have been such a seeker. I have done so many seminars, retreats, workshops and classes. I've read a plethora of self-help books, seeking something and never quite finding it, like an elusive itch that you just can't quite scratch. I only found relief when I found the truth at the core of my very own being. That's why I was passionate about telling Carolanne's story and writing this book. I believe it is your ticket to awakening and remembering the truth of your power.

I've realized that in order to thrive, you have to bring your whole self to the table. The only way to show up with your whole self it to awaken to your whole power. Carolanne and I both continually and actively do this work on ourselves. Any time life throws a curveball or even an unexpected blow to the head, we go back to the work of transformation. Every curveball, every shitty situation life serves, is a call to self-awakening. This book is full of the tools you will need to unlock the codes to your potential and unleash your superpowers.

Make no mistake: we're not flippantly doling out inner peace and self-love like Tootsie Rolls. We're inviting you to do the work of transformation in order to wake up to your own truth, and to gain more peace and love in the experiences of your life. We hope you're not easily offended. Don't take this stuff too seriously. We're here to have fun. Transformation doesn't have to be tough, somber or ultra-serious. It's an adventure. So check your judging little voices at the door, and brace yourself. Our commitment is to bring you the best of what we have lived and learned, and to bring it with love.

It is time to wake up to the awareness of the brilliant, shining light that you really are. It's time to come back to yourself. I know it sounds a little woo-woo and intangible, at least right now. As we move along this journey, we will make your understanding of these topics more concrete with simple, real life application. No watered down, westernized pseudo-mysticism here. We'll provide a simple and functional blueprint for transformation, a powerful set of tools for your spiritual toolbox to help you awaken your inner potential, and awaken to the truth of your own power. It's so simple, so easy, so accessible with immediate, profound results. You'll see.

We see your light, every single one of you. Just like every human on the planet, you have some junk inside that muddies up your light. Some have more than others, but that's okay– it's just part of the human experience. On this journey we will pinpoint what, when and where experiences have muddied up your energy and teach you how to transform and transmute it, therefore transcending it. You are a powerhouse of energy. We're just going to help you find where it's snagged up and stuck. Then we'll help you to unstick it. Imagine what you can do when you reclaim that kind of energy: Manifest your dreams and desires. Experience pure joy and passion in life. Heal yourself. Heal the planet. Make miracles happen. The possibilities are limitless. So is your potential.

STRUCTURE OF THIS BOOK
I love numbers and the meanings of numbers. Numbers are powerful symbolic expressions of life. Numbers are connected to all things in nature, and people have used numbers since the beginning of time as representations of universal principles.

This book is exactly thirteen chapters long. That's by intention and design. The first twelve chapters set the stage and give you some background information, with each chapter building on the one before. Twelve is a significant number, and the first twelve chapters give you significant information. The number twelve represents a completed cycle of experience. It's also symbolic of the creation of the universe and the division of unity or God into twelve individual and distinct vibrations or tones. We've seen the number twelve repeated throughout our planet's history: in Judaism, there are the twelve sons of Jacob who formed the twelve tribes of Israel; there are twelve signs of the zodiac; there are twelve months in a year; there are twelve hours of day and twelve hours of night; Jesus had twelve disciples; there were twelve knights at the round table; Buddha had twelve followers and Buddhists believe life is composed of twelve stages; the Greeks believed in twelve gods on Mount Olympus; Even measurements are based on the number twelve: a dozen is twelve of something, a shilling is twelve pence, and a foot is twelve inches.

The number thirteen is symbolic of upheaval, destruction and death, making way for the breaking of new ground so that you may birth yourself anew. The number thirteen is the doorway to a higher level of expression and experience. When you complete a cycle on the spiral of life, you jump up to the next rung. The number thirteen represents the doorway to that next level. Thirteen is the doorway to transformation, the end of something old, a rebirth and renewal.

Twelve symbolizes a complete cycle. It invites us to move forward to the number thirteen, which represents a doorway to a new level. There are twelve months in a year, then a new year begins. There are twelve signs of the zodiac, then it starts a new cycle. There are twelve chapters of foundational information in this book. Chapter thirteen opens the door to a new level of consciousness. Thirteen is an invitation to wake up to the awareness of the brilliant shining light that you really are, a doorway to remembering your organic truth. Chapter thirteen reveals the HEAL Technique®, a simple technique on the cutting edge of healing that will help you to unlock your own codes to understanding the truth of who you really are. The HEAL Technique® is the doorway to your personal power. By using it, you will learn the easiest way to shift and transform.

In the spirit of love, names and personal details throughout the book have been changed for a few reasons: to keep confidentiality, protect privacy, and provide anonymity. We are hugely grateful for the opportunity to tell the stories of Carolanne's clients, very personal stories of healing and transformation, by using pretend names. Their stories are the human story. Their journeys mirror the journey we are all on— the journey of human experience, transformation and awakening.

The information in this book is based upon the research and the personal and professional experiences of the authors. It is not intended as a substitute for traditional medical or psychological diagnosis and treatment. Spiritual healing and energy work are not substitutes for traditional medical treatment. If you have a serious health imbalance, please consult with your doctor or other appropriate health care professional, and make complementary healing part of a complete health care program. Results are not guaranteed. The authors are not responsible for any adverse effects or consequences resulting from the use of any of the suggestions or techniques discussed in this book. The intent of the authors is only to offer information of a general nature to help you in your journey to total well-being.

CONTENTS

1) YOU ARE POWERFUL: *Claim Your Power*

THE GIFT

Carolanne couldn't open her eyes or wiggle her fingers. She tried her toes—nothing. Her whole body was completely paralyzed. Panic had taken up residence in every crevice of her unfeeling body. She couldn't feel her body there on the operating table, but she could acutely feel every ounce of panic and visceral terror within it. How was that even possible? She felt the doctors move a breathing tube down her throat. She wanted more than anything to open her mouth and scream, but the connection between her brain and body had become a one-way uplink of pain and terror. There was no outgoing connection. No matter how intensely she willed it, she had no way to let them know she was awake. It was a nightmare of the worst kind, like being trapped inside of a corpse with no way out. It was pure living hell.

Her awareness was jolted and her attention moved to the stabbing pain in her abdomen. It was the laparoscope. It felt like a searing hot poker penetrating her insides, and there was nothing she could do to protect herself. Primal fear coursed through her veins where there should have been anesthetic. Next came a puncture in what must have been her bellybutton. Her abdomen was being insufflated with carbon dioxide gas. This was to elevate the abdominal wall above her internal organs like a dome, so the doctors could perform the surgery with ease. She didn't care about that right now. She was being blown up like a balloon and it was excruciating. The tightness in her abdomen was so intense and the pressure was so violent that she was sure she would explode. She literally felt like she might detonate and blow up from the inside, leaving a storm of blood and guts on the operating table without so much as a yelp.

Then, mercifully, she blacked out. This happened only briefly, but it was sweet, temporary relief. Her consciousness swam between a state of awakened, paralyzed terror and the respite of unconsciousness. When she could hold on to consciousness long enough, in addition to being hyperaware of the pressure and pain in her abdomen, she realized that she had her hearing back. Before, she only had one sense– the sense of stark, unadulterated pain. Now that she had her sense of hearing, she focused all of her attention on it, listening closely and trying to patch together what was going on. She tuned in to the voices, and recognized the modulated voice of her doctor. No discerning insights came to her, however. She just heard the doctors talking about a dinner they were going to at a local restaurant that evening. They were making small talk about the dishes they enjoyed there, and speculating on what they might order for dinner later.

Then, Carolanne blacked out again. This time, she floated right out of her battered body and felt light and at peace. Other than lightness and peacefulness, she did not go through any of the typical and awesome out-of-body or near-death experience phenomena aside from being able to momentarily escape the EXCRUCIATING, AGONIZING, UNBEARABLE, PIERCING, TRAUMATIC, INSUFFERABLE, TORMENTING, TOE-CURLING-IF-ONLY-HER-TOES-COULD-MOVE PAIN. There were no greetings from dead relatives, no angels, no big tunnel of light.

As she was peacefully floating in this blissful state, she heard a voice. This was not a voice that she heard with her ears, nor was it the disembodied voice of a spirit. It was her own voice, an internal voice. It said, "Here is a gift for you." Then she had a vision. It was a vision of a gift, only it wasn't in a big box tied with a pretty red ribbon. It was wrapped in a handkerchief attached to a stick. Right then, she didn't give a damn about the gift. She just wanted this nightmare to end.

And very soon it did.

After returning home post operation, Carolanne woke up the next morning and remembered the voice, the vision and the strangely packaged gift. She pulled back the covers, her feet dangling over the side of the bed, and made the pivotal and life-altering decision to live. That was the beginning of Carolanne's journey of awakening. That was the beginning of her gift of power to herself. That was the genesis of her healing.

It was only a couple weeks before that surgery that her doctor told her to get her affairs in order because her organs were shutting down. At the time, Carolanne was just thirty-one years old and this was the umpteenth time she was in the hospital for her umpteenth surgery. That surgery was the last, because what followed that experience was an awakening into true power. In that moment after surgery, Carolanne made the decision that she would live, that she would not leave her children motherless. Just by the power of that decisive moment alone, Carolanne claimed sovereignty over her life and wellness. The universe opened up to her. Her journey of power and healing had begun.

YOU ARE POWERFUL

You are a powerful, magnificent being. So many of us look outside of ourselves for answers to the questions of the universe, not realizing that all of the answers, all of the wisdom, all of the power lies within. Workshops, retreats and gurus might be fun, but they are only necessary to the extent that they are able to remind you of your own innate power. They are only useful if they lead you back to the center of yourself.

Every saint and sage from the beginning of time has attempted to enlighten us with this truth. Jesus proclaimed, "The kingdom of God is within you."[3] The Buddha said, "The way is not in the sky. The way is in the heart." The truth of our immeasurable power is a teaching that is universal and timeless. Every great religion of the world, every spiritual tradition, every wisdom tradition has attempted to help us come to know this ultimate, simple and elegant truth about ourselves–that we are more powerful than we know, and that all of that power lies right in the center of our beings.

Before anyone gets defensive, let's pause here for a minute to address this supercharged word: God. There are many names for this energy: Source, God, the Universe, Universal Mind, Supreme Intelligence, Consciousness, Spirit, Allah, Christ, Brahman, the Tao, Om, the Great Void, Creator, the Field, Intention, the Great I Am, the Supreme Architect, Higher Power, Divine Intelligence, the Force, Nature, the Divine, the Light... Whatever you call this energy, we mean to be inclusive in this book of that name and all names, because it's all God. There is no place that God is not. In fact, trying to define God is diminishing to the experience of God. God is indescribable, indefinable, infinite, and beyond description.

We are not talking about religion. We are not talking about doctrine or dogma. Attachment to those things has a tendency to keep you dependent upon them, reaching outside of yourself for the divine. We are talking about becoming liberated, in order to trust your own inner voice. The aim of this book is to connect with God's voice inside of you.

When I was a little girl, my favorite book was *God is Love*, a sweet little yellow book gifted to me by my Aunt Myrtice when I was about three years old. I don't remember much about the contents except the pretty little pictures, but the title stuck with me. Little did I know that I would spend the next several decades seeking the experience of God, when the answer was there with me all along in that raggedy old crayon-art-covered children's book. *God is love.*

My favorite definition of God that I have ever heard was when Panache Desai appeared on *Super Soul Sunday*.[4] Oprah asked him, "What is God?" He answered with... nothing. Pure silence. I thought this was brilliant. There are no words.

I once went to a workshop led by American self-help author and motivational speaker Wayne Dyer. I loved the way he explained God and our relationship to God. He explained that God is like the ocean. If you take a cup of the ocean, you have a glass of God. It's not as big and maybe not as strong, but it's altogether God. If you take that glass of ocean water and pour it out on the grass, it will evaporate and change form, going back out into air, into the clouds, then back to its source. While it's separated from Source, *that's the ego.* That is the part of us that believes we are separate, that we are what we do, what we have, and what we accomplish, that we are our reputations, and that we are separate from everyone else. It is the illusion of the self. When we feel we are separate from God, we lose the power of God. When we return back to our Source, we gain all the power of Source. The thing is, we were never really separate. *We were part of Source all along.*

We are connected to Source always, we just forget. Our egos tell us we are separate, and our programming tells us we are separate. The truth is, we are always connected to God. We feel separate from this field of energy when we drop into a low vibration. To connect to our seat of power, it is as simple as cleansing our connecting link to Source and unsticking the trapped energy that blocks us from being the highest expression of ourselves. We are Source energy.

As part of Source energy, we are powerful. The latest scientific discoveries are beginning to give evidence of the energetic power at the very core of our being. In Dr. Masaru Emoto's experiment, *The Hidden Messages in Water*, he projected different vibrational patterns through thoughts, words and music onto water and then froze them, turning the patterns into ice crystals. Using a powerful microscope and high-speed photography in a very cold room, Dr. Emoto discovered physical evidence that our thoughts and feelings–our vibrational frequencies–affect physical reality. Water exposed to high vibrational energy in the form of written words and phrases such as "love," "love and gratitude" and "I love you" created beautiful, complex, symmetrical and complete snowflake patterns. In contrast, water exposed to low vibrational frequencies in the form of written words and phrases such as "I hate you" formed incomplete, disorganized, malformed and asymmetrical patterns with dull colors.[5]

Since our bodies are seventy-five percent water, it's important to consider how our vibrational frequencies may be affecting our physical bodies. If our energetic vibration is powerful enough to change the crystalline structure of water, what else might we be impacting?

The truth is... EVERYTHING.

THE POWER OF NOW

Now is the time for remembering the truth of who you are. Now is the time for coming into your power. After all, it's your birthright. In fact, it's the birthright of every human soul on the planet. The sooner you shift into this knowingness, the sooner all of humanity may shift. We're all collectively on the verge of a momentous tipping point, a critical mass. It's the hundredth monkey effect, a phenomenon discussed by Dr. Lyall Watson in his book *Lifetide*, in which a spontaneous leap of consciousness occurs by unexplained, supernatural or energetic means from a small select few to the whole collective.[6] Congratulations! You've been chosen as one of the select few. We're beginning to tip, so get ready.

In 1952, on the island of Koshima, Japan, scientists fed sweet potatoes to monkeys. The monkeys loved them, but didn't like the sand they were covered in. One day, a monkey named Imo realized she could wash the sand off the sweet potatoes in a nearby stream. Thrilled, she taught her mother and some of her monkey playmates. Then her monkey buddies taught their mommies, too. Between 1952 and 1958, all the little monkeys on Koshima Island were joyfully washing the sand off their sweet potatoes. Then, something startling happened. In the fall of 1958, when about one hundred Koshima monkeys had adopted the practice of sweet potato washing, the entire tribe simultaneously joined in. The added energy of this hundredth monkey created the pivotal tipping point in consciousness. This occurred not just on Koshima Island, but *everywhere*. Colonies of monkeys on other islands and the mainland suddenly began washing their sweet potatoes as well.[7]

You see, when a critical mass of individuals achieves a new level of awareness or a new state of consciousness, this new way of being creates a tipping point *en masse*. The added energy of the hundredth monkey somehow created a breakthrough, a ripple effect in the consciousness of the rest of the monkey tribe. When a certain critical number achieves awareness, this new awareness is then communicated from mind to mind. We are on the cusp of our own hundredth monkey phenomenon in the consciousness of humankind. One of you reading right now might be that hundredth monkey that creates the tipping point, the breakthrough. You might be that one last person who tunes in to this awareness of our inherent organic power. Through this awareness, the field may be strengthened exponentially, such that this knowing and reclaiming of personal power may ripple through all of humanity on the planet. We are living in very exciting times, indeed.

Spirituality is the personal experience of the divine. It's the experience of feeling unconditionally loved, so much and so powerfully that you are filled up to overflowing. You are so full of love that you want to–that you can't help but–love others unconditionally. This is what the shift is all about.

The shift is happening right now. We're right in the midst of it. For this planet to shift into a higher vibration, it requires more individuals to awaken. As the result of your shift, many will feel your vibrational changes and begin to shift themselves. Your energetic frequency impacts all aspects of your life… and far beyond. You are more powerful than you can imagine.

Not only are you super powerful, you also already have all the codes required to understand the truth of who you really are. Now is the time, more than ever before, to understand your organic truth, to understand why you are here, and to get down to the business of transformation. It is time to begin unlocking your personal codes, and cultivating the spiritual tools for the next phase of your journey.

Now is the time to reclaim your power and find your place in the divine puzzle, so that you can fulfill what you came here to do. Now is the time to create an alignment with the truth of who you are, in a deep, rich and fulfilling way. The only way to do that is to awaken to your organic power. Claim and own your power. Now is a critical juncture in time. A perfect storm of conditions currently exists in the world, requiring us to make a choice as to whether or not we will embrace new discoveries, whether or not we will awaken to our inherent power and embrace it.

This is a book about healing and transformation, but the irony is that you don't need it. You are not broken. You don't need to be healed. You might just need a reminder of the power within you. A nudge. Or a kick in the ass. Let this book be that for you.

There are no design flaws in the divine. Your life's blueprint does not have to contain pain or suffering or trauma. Your life's path is yours. The plan is going to unfold no matter what. How you choose to experience it is up to you. You can experience a low expression of yourself and a low vibration of your path, or you can live the highest, fullest expression of yourself and live the highest expression of your path. You've allowed yourself to believe that you are broken, that you need fixing, that you need healing, that life is hard, that you are not enough, and that you have limitations. These are all programs– conditioning of the world in which we live. You are not your programs. You can change your programs at the energetic source. It's time to reprogram, baby.

You are an unlimited being condensed down into physical form. You think the information you perceive with your senses is the whole of reality, but that's simply not true. The realm of the senses is so limited. We can only see between the ranges of infrared light and ultraviolet light. We can only hear within a certain limited decibel range. We can't hear at the ultrasonic range of a dog whistle because it is above the range of human hearing, but we don't doubt its existence since we can easily see and measure that dogs hear it. We know our sense of smell is limited in comparison to that of our canine friends. On the flipside, dogs don't see color and we do. Perhaps little Fido would doubt the existence of red, green, yellow and orange because his senses are limited to black and white, but we know a whole array of colors exists because we trust our senses. But should we? Just as Fido can't see purple, we must consider what data we are missing out on because our senses are so limited.

Many of us think the whole of reality is what we can comprehend through the limited instrument of the senses, but the full scope of reality goes far beyond what we can perceive. We live in the realm of the senses, and that information is filtered through our minds. The mind is flawed by programming.

Case in point: Some religions teach that we have fallen from grace, that we are sinners, and that we need redemption from a source outside of ourselves. This perpetuates the myth that we are inherently flawed, which perpetuates a program that instructs us to seek salvation. These are actually programs to keep people in their place, and to keep the powers that be in power. They are not truth. They may seem like truth right now because we have been subject to messages for our entire lives that tell us this is "truth." If you really examine this "truth," and look into the center of your own being, you may find a different answer.

Still not convinced? Check your programming on this one: The story of evolution by the forces of mutation and natural selection has been perpetuated by our education system and culture. Charles Darwin's *The Origin of Species* is the foundation of this narrative.[8] The story goes something like this: Resources such as food are limited. As populations grow, there is a struggle for survival. Individuals who are less suited to the environment are less likely to survive and less likely to reproduce. They eventually die off. Individuals who are better suited to the environment are more likely to survive and more likely to reproduce. When they do, they leave their heritable traits to future generations. Over time, this leads to adaptation, mutation and the evolution of populations. This is natural selection.

This is a very specific narrative that we have inherited. Did you know the ideas of natural selection and survival of the fittest comprised just a fraction of Darwin's work on evolution? In actuality, based on Darwin's work, nature is based on a model of cooperation and mutual aid, not violent competition. In fact, the bulk of Darwin's work discussed the importance of cooperation in a species' survival. However, the well-known concept of survival of the fittest has been peddled since the late nineteenth century, and is still the widespread belief today. Why?

The answer is programming: To keep us in a program of scarcity and competition, and to focus on selfishness as the driving force of human nature. We've been bombarded with this narrative of natural selection for almost two hundred years. We've heard it so frequently that most of us have accepted it as truth. It's in our books, movies, video games and TV shows.

During the latter part of his life, Darwin published *The Descent of Man* in an effort to pull together his ideas on human evolution.[9] Because *The Origin of Species* was focused entirely on pre-human evolution, Darwin sought to address human evolution in this work at the end of his life. Despite its publication, *The Origin of Species* is the work we hear about most frequently. His work on human evolution has been largely ignored. Why? *Programming.*

In *The Descent of Man*, Darwin presents an evolved theory of evolution that goes well beyond random mutation or survival of the fittest and accounts for the rise of family, community, cooperation, morality and love. Darwin himself says that he "perhaps attributed too much to the action of natural selection or survival of the fittest."[10] I don't know about you, but I never learned about that in biology or history class. It's largely been kept hidden. I don't mean that in a paranoid conspiracy theorist kind of way. It just has not been the particular narrative that we have been told at a basic level. The story of competition won out over the story of cooperation and love. But I have to wonder, what if the latter was the driving narrative? We'd surely be living in a different world.

Award-winning author and internationally known evolutionary systems scientist David Loye speculates in his book *Darwin's Lost Theory of Love* that the focus on competition and survival of the fittest has contributed to some of the deadliest wars in history.[11] Loye reveals in his analysis of *The Descent of Man* that what moves evolution forward is love.

We need to reframe the narrative that we tell ourselves about who we are and where we're going. I don't accept the belief that we have fallen. Instead, I believe we are rising. We are evolving, and this evolution is driven by the force of love. We are right on the cusp of the next level of evolution. It begins with our consciousness. It begins with love. First, we must get beyond the programming. We need to popularize a different message, a message of love.

Remembering the truth of who you are is the catalyst that will open up your capacity for self-love. Self-love is the driving force behind creating a deeply satisfying and fulfilling life that's in alignment with the truth of who you are. Let's remove the energetic blocks so you can remember and access your authentic truth, so you can embrace who you are, so you can be free to be who you were created to be: Powerful. Unlimited. Balanced. Joyful. Loved. Loving. Creative. Perfect. Imperfect. Human. Divine.

When you find the divine within the cells of your own being, you will know that God breathes within everyone else on the planet, too. Your quest to dig deeper will lead you to go wider, too, in connection with the rest of the human tribe.

Take a journey straight into your heart that will help you to remember the brilliant, magnificent being that you are. You know your soul has been trying to wake up to this truth. Your life has been speaking to you at every moment. Of course, you get it conceptually. That's nothing compared to what will happen when you really wake up to this truth through the experiences of your life. If you could see your power, it would be awe-inspiring. Your jaw would drop and you'd get up and do the victory dance. The problem is, you can't always see it. That is, at least not right away in this reality. Or perhaps, like most of us, you know conceptually that you are powerful beyond measure but don't know how to access or unleash that power. You know that you have a ton of potential inside but you're not able to fully unleash it. It's like all the good stuff is locked inside and you can't find the key.

We know. We've felt the same way. Now that we've found the key, we're giving it to you with a double scoop of love.

2) YOU ARE ENERGY: *Everything is Energetic*

What's going on in your life that you don't understand? What do you want to heal or change? What would you like to create or manifest? What is keeping you from manifesting those things in this reality? What's blocking you from living to your highest potential? What's got you feeling stuck, or not quite in alignment with your life's purpose? Whatever it is, it's energetic in nature.

Everything in the universe is energy. All of life is energy. Quantum physics has shown that everything in the world around us is comprised of vibrating packets of energy. Magnify our cells down to tiny little atoms and you would see that we are made up of subtle energy fields. We may appear to be made from solid matter, but looks can be deceiving. Put particles in a particle accelerator, set them spinning and make them collide to try and identify the source, and you would discover what Einstein knew to be true: There is no particle at the source, there is pure, unbounded energy vibrating so fast it defies measurement.[12]

In fact, Einstein had a lot to say about energy. Einstein said, "There is no essential distinction between mass and energy. Energy has mass and mass represents energy."[13] His famous equation, $E=mc^2$, revealed matter and energy to be interchangeable forms of the exact same thing. He said there are not two fundamental physical entities–one material (matter) and another immaterial (energy)–but only one: *energy*.

In his book *What We Talk About When We Talk About God*, American author and pastor Rob Bell explains this concept well: "Matter is locked-up energy, and energy is liberated matter."[14] At the most basic level, you are energy vibrating in a larger field of energy. We live in a vibrational universe. We are vibrationally alive in this sea of infinite energy, each with our own unique vibrational frequency.

Everything is energy. This is not philosophy or new age psychobabble. This is physics. Discoveries in quantum physics are now providing evidence that this is a vibrational universe. Since everything is energy and you are a part of everything, you are also energy. So are your thoughts, emotions, wishes, and desires, the things you want to change, heal and transform, and the experiences or things you want to manifest and create. The causes of disease, depression, scarcity, anxiety, and unhappiness are also energetic. All of these things have an energetic source, and impact your energetic frequency. Your energetic frequency impacts everything in your life– the people around you, the circumstances of your life, and the reality you experience. Everything. There is nothing that it does not touch.

What this means is that you have POWER! Astounding, enormous, extraordinary power, and limitless, unbounded, superhuman potential. As you know from every superhero story ever told, with great power comes great responsibility. It's no different with your very own superhero story. Yes, yours is a superhero story, too.

Here are the facts:

You are freaking powerful. You are so powerful that the entire chapter to follow gushes on and on about the powerful, magnificent creature that you are. And it still doesn't even begin to scratch the surface of the powerhouse that is within the core of your being. Not even a little tiny bit.

You–*and only you*–are responsible for your life. It doesn't matter what your mama, daddy or ex-boyfriend did to you. It doesn't matter where you come from, what you had or what you didn't have. It doesn't matter if life handed you a golden ticket or a shit sandwich. Nobody but you is responsible for your life. You are responsible for the energy that you create for yourself, and the energy you bring to every single moment of your life.

Dr. Jill Bolte Taylor, a Harvard-educated brain scientist, suffered a stroke in the left hemisphere of her brain at the age of thirty-seven. After eight years of recovery she published *My Stroke of Insight*, which details her miraculous and enlightening journey of healing.[15] With the deterioration of the left side of her brain, she lost her ego and language centers. She lost the ability to talk, walk, read, write, categorize, organize, judge and analyze. She couldn't remember the details of her life. She couldn't remember her loved ones. She couldn't even remember her own mother. She couldn't experience herself as separate. She couldn't experience *anything* as separate. All she could perceive was the present moment, and the connection of all things. She felt at one with the universe. With her left brain's neural circuitry blown, her consciousness could only perceive energy.

When caregivers, doctors and nurses would walk into the room, Dr. Taylor could not identify or recognize them. She could not communicate with or understand them. But she could perceive their energy. From her right-brain consciousness, she knew exactly who had her best interests at heart, who believed she would make a recovery, and whose energy supported her healing. All she could feel was their energy; their invisible expression of vibrational frequency was the only thing her right brain could grasp. Through that experience, she understood how important it is for all of us to take responsibility for the energy we bring to all moments of our lives, and the energy we allow into our lives.

All of life is energy. Although you may not be able to see it, it's always there. What the eye can see is a very narrow and limited band of the electromagnetic spectrum called visible light. Most of what is happening in this vastly alive and vibrational universe is happening outside of the spectrum of what we can see with our eyes. We are energetic beings. Yes, we have physical bodies, but we have a luminous energy field–sometimes called the biofield–that extends beyond the physical body. In truth, what this means is that you are an energy being that happens to spill over into a physical realm. This electromagnetic field of ours informs and organizes the physical body. The energy field surrounding our body is a torus– a donut-shaped energy vortex with a narrow hole in the center. The energy flows in through our feet, up through our bodies and out the tops of our heads, expanding and circulating around our bodies and back up through our feet again. It's a self-sustaining, self-perpetuating energy pattern.

From this energetic field, we are transmitting our personal energetic frequency at every single moment. Once you understand that it is your personal energetic frequency that creates the reality that you experience, you are empowered to take responsibility for it. Take responsibility for the energy you are pulling in, up and around your toroidal electromagnetic field, and take responsibility for the vibrations you are feeding out into the universe. Each person's toroidal energy field is unique, but each person's field is open and connected to every other energy field in an expansive sea of infinite energy. We're beaming little signals in every instant, informing the universe with our personal energetic frequency, and the universe is responding in kind. If you don't like what shows up in your life, change your energy. The outside world is just a reflection of your internal condition. You can change the energy, and change your life in the process. Change your frequency, and get a different result. In fact, changing at the vibrational level is the supreme level of transformation because it is the source. This invisible energy field is what organizes all of our reality.

If you're like most people, you probably already understand that your vibration creates your life. What you really want to know is what creates your energetic vibration and how to raise it. That's what this book is all about: encoding yourself and your life with the highest vibrational frequency of all, the frequency of unconditional love. There is no higher expression. Our intention for this book is to help you awaken to this expression of love in your daily life; to live from your heart and place of authentic power; to live your organic truth; *to be love in manifest form.*

If you have a physical ailment, illness or disease, your doctors are likely prescribing drugs. That only addresses the physical, and often masks the symptoms without addressing the cause. All causes are energetic in nature. This book will guide you through a simple process called the HEAL Technique®, which dives straight to the source of the trauma and removes it, without the drama. It's quick, easy, painless and effective. You'll learn how to clear the stagnant energy that's lodged and festering inside of you, by transforming it so that energy can flow.

When energy flows, new doors open. When energy flows, new neurons and neural pathways are built in the brain. When energy flows, you open channels in the brain for new information to flow. You gain the highest possible perspective. You can contemplate a new direction for yourself. You can see the possibilities and open up to creativity in order to manifest your potential.

It's time to prepare for a new way of being. It's time to wake up to the awareness of the powerful being that you really are. Claim true responsibility for every aspect of your life. Uncover your subconscious programming and put an end to the repeating patterns that block you from experiencing your authentic power. Learn to feel your way through patterns that shape your life, so you can find freedom by breaking the ones that no longer serve you. Reclaim lost energy that you have given away to programs, situations and people that don't serve your highest good, or don't keep you in the frequency of love. Learn how to get out of your head and into your heart, so that you can awaken into your organic truth and begin to live your grandest vision for your life. It's time to come back to yourself, your truest, most whole self, and to discover the highest expression of your truest, most whole self.

This book will lead you on a journey towards doing just that. Inside your being, you possess the codes to heal and transform yourself and your life. These are your personal codes for unlocking your personal power, the truth of who you really are.

3) YOU ARE STUCK: *Unstick Your Energy*

"What would you like to focus on shifting in your session today?" Carolanne asked in her characteristic sunshiny way.

"Cervical cancer," Jodi responded, teary-eyed, her voice quavering. "Oh, plus an obstructed bowel. You know. Just in case the cancer wasn't enough." Carolanne knew she was trying to be funny but the despondent look in Jodi's eyes betrayed her.

Jodi was a thirty-six-year-old mother who had been diagnosed with stage two cervical cancer. She looked incredibly thin and frail. She revealed to Carolanne that she was not eating. Lack of appetite and a bowel obstruction were peeling off the pounds. She had one child, a five-year-old boy named Jamison, and desperately wanted to have another. Despite the yearning she felt to give Jamison a baby brother or sister, there were a lot of obstacles in her way.

For starters, there was the cancer. She was just too sick to get pregnant or carry a baby to term. The unspoken question was, would she live long enough to raise a child even if she could get pregnant and deliver to term? In order to keep the cancer from spreading and to increase her odds of survival, her doctor wanted her to have a hysterectomy.

Cervical cancer was not her only physical ailment. She also had a bowel obstruction triggered by scar tissue that was causing tremendous belly pain, severe bloating, and a serious poop apprehension. This, in turn, caused a real disinclination to eat. And you can't grow a human without eating.

On top of the health-related hurdles on her mommy path, Jodi's marriage was on the rocks. She and her husband had steadily been growing apart since her diagnosis. At a time when she needed his rock solid support and comfort the most, he became distant and withdrawn. Her husband was as cold as ice when she needed warmth like a newborn baby in the middle of a North Dakota winter. She'd secretly thought about separation, but couldn't bear the thought of another area of her life falling apart. But it already was. Her whole life was completely falling apart. She felt like she was falling to pieces.

Carolanne could see she was in complete despair. A lifelong empath, her heart ached for Jodi. So they got right down to business.

Carolanne began by calibrating her starting vibration. This is basically an energetic "before" picture. As you can imagine, Jodi's starting vibration revealed that she was depressed and angry. Carolanne calibrated a few more vibrational measurements, and then they dug deep into the fun stuff: *emotions.*

"Close your eyes and put your hands on your heart. Feel into your cancer. Feel into this obstruction in your bowel. Feel into all the feelings you have related to the imbalances in your physical body. How does it make you *feel?*" Carolanne started the excavation of emotions, putting emphasis on the word *feel.*

"Scared," Jodi responded quietly with her eyes still closed, her right hand over her heart and her left hand over her right.

"What's the intensity of that feeling on a scale of zero to ten, with ten being the highest?" Carolanne asked.

"Ten," Jodi answered without hesitation.

"When you feel into the feeling of being scared, how does that make you feel?" Carolanne continued.

"Powerless," Jodi answered.

"What's the intensity, zero to ten?"

"Umm... eight," she estimated.

"Now peel back the feeling of powerlessness. What's underneath the feeling of being powerless?" Carolanne carried on the process of digging up layer after layer of energy and emotion, and rating the intensity of it. The dialog volleyed back and forth like a ping-pong match.

"Guilt, guilt and more guilt. I don't want to leave my son behind without a mother."

"What's the intensity, zero to ten?"

"Nine or ten."

"What's under the feelings of guilt?"

"I'm terrified."

"What's the intensity?"

"Nine."

"What's under the feeling of being terrified?"

"Anger!"

"Zero to ten?"

"Ten."

"When you feel angry, how does that make you feel?"

"Depressed."

"Intensity?"

"Seven."

"What's under depression?"

"Exhaustion."

"Rate it."

"Seven."

"When you feel exhausted, how does that make you feel?"

"Lonely. I feel so alone." Jodi's voice trembled. Carolanne knew they were getting somewhere now, as the energy of the emotion bubbled up to the surface.

"What's the intensity?"

Jodi's lip quivered as she answered, "Nine."

"Really feel into that loneliness. Now, lift it up and peek underneath. Can you tell me what is under that feeling of loneliness and being alone?"

"I'm scared," Jodi said as she opened her eyes, realizing she had come full circle back to the very first emotion that she had identified in this process. A long exhale escaped her lips.

"Gooooooood," Carolanne cooed reassuringly. "Now, let's look into the energy and emotion around your marriage. Allow your eyes to close again. Hands back on your heart." Jodi did what she was instructed to do as Carolanne continued to guide her.

"Now, when you feel into the energy of your marriage, of feeling distant from your husband, of him being withdrawn from you... how does that make you feel?"

"Scared. I don't want to lose him."

"What's the intensity?"

"It's intense. Probably a ten."

"Mm-hmm. And when you feel into the feelings of being scared, of losing him, what feelings come up for you?"

"I feel powerless. It doesn't matter what I say or do, he is pulling further and further away and I can't stop it. He won't talk to me. I feel invisible." Despair dripped from every word.

"Rate the intensity."

"Seven or eight."

"And what does powerless and invisible feel like to you?"

"I feel guilty for feeling that way. Like I've already given up."

"Intensity?"

"Eight or nine."

"You're doing great, Jodi. Now peel back the feelings of guilt… what's underneath?"

"I'm terrified! There's nothing I can do! It's terrifying!" Jodi's voice went up a couple decibels. Serious energy was being stirred up.

"Zero to ten?"

"Eight."

"Yes. Terrified. And how does that make you feel?" She was going through the motions of asking the questions to allow Jodi to move through the process of finding the emotions surrounding her distress in her marriage, but Carolanne knew what would come next. Depression. The pattern of energy in the breakdown of her marriage was exactly the same as the energetic pattern of the breakdown of her body. Intensities varied a little, but the pattern was the same. It was the same pattern that was in her DNA. That's why it kept showing up.

"Depressed."

"Rate it."

"Nine."

"And what's underneath the depression?" *Exhaustion.*

"Exhaustion."

"Yeeeeesssss," Carolanne crooned. She loved the elegance and flow of the patterns of the universe. It was always predictable, graceful and simple, even when it looked like chaos on the surface. "And what's the intensity of that exhaustion?"

"Eight."

"What does exhaustion feel like to you?" *Loneliness was up to bat next.*

"Total isolation. Complete loneliness." Jodi's voice echoed the melancholy she was feeling.

"Zero to ten?"

"Ten."

"When you feel into that complete loneliness and total isolation, how does that make you feel?" *Scared was up to take a swing at bat and Carolanne knew it would be a home run.*

"Scared," Jodi whispered in the smallest, slightest voice. Then, without another word or breath, her eyes fluttered open. She must have sensed the energetic home run on some level of her being as well.

"Jodi, what you've essentially just told me is that you've been running a pattern of energy that has shown up in both your physical body and in your relationship with your husband. Scared. Powerless. Terrified. Guilty. Angry. Depressed. Exhausted. Lonely. You've been running that pattern over and over and over again in different areas of your life for a very, very long time now. Feeling lonely is at the root of it all. Lonely has been feeding energy to Exhausted. Exhausted has been feeding Depression. Depression in turn fed Angry, which fed Guilty, which fed Terrified, which fed Powerless, which fed Scared, all the way up the energetic food chain."

Ding-ding-ding-ding-DING! Profound realization lit up Jodi's face. She had found her codes! Carolanne adored those a-ha moments of insight and transformation. But they weren't done yet. They still had to find the origination point, the essential big bang that set that particular energetic pattern into motion in Jodi's life, spiraling time after time, manifesting as relationship issues and illness. Those manifestations were a call to something greater: to awakening to her power, and to claiming the power to heal and clear them.

"Close your eyes and put your hands on your heart. Really feel into that root emotion of loneliness. Tell me… where are you storing it in your body?" Carolanne asked quietly.

"I don't know," Jodi responded.

"Pretend that you do. Just tune in to your body. Feel the loneliness in your body. Where is it? It might feel like a tightness somewhere, or perhaps an ache, or even a hollowness somewhere in your body. Feel it. You might even hear an answer or see it on the movie screen of your mind. Where is that loneliness in your body?" she asked again.

"In my abdomen," Jodi answered after a brief pause.

"Good work, Jodi," Carolanne encouraged. "In a moment, I'm going to count backwards from five to one. When I do, a memory is going to pop into your mind. This will be a memory from a time when you first felt that feeling of loneliness. Five... four... three... two... one. What's the memory?"

"I'm sixteen years old. I'm pregnant... four months pregnant. I didn't even realize I was pregnant for so long. I remember being so shocked. I couldn't believe I was pregnant because I had only had sex the one time," Jodi said as she recalled the events that had taken place two decades earlier.

"Mm-hmmm," Carolanne encouraged.

"I remember looking at the calendar and counting the weeks backwards to the time I went out with David– that was the guy. The, um, father. It was the one and only time I had sex, so it wasn't difficult to figure out. It was exactly sixteen weeks prior, the last day of the school year. I never told him. Or anyone, for that matter. Until now..." Jodi's voice trailed off, lost in the memory. She was silent for a full minute and a half, trying to release the overwhelming burden of keeping a secret of that magnitude for twenty years.

"You didn't tell your parents?" Carolanne prompted, knowing it was important to get her talking again. This was to keep the energy flowing, to allow her to process the memory out loud and to get her on the path of clearing it.

"No. They were going through a divorce. They were always fighting. It was so stressful."

"So, what happened?" Carolanne nudged gently.

"Well, at sixteen weeks it was too late to have an abortion. I couldn't tell my parents. I didn't want to tell David. I didn't know who to talk to. I didn't know what to do. I was so worried and anxious that I just stopped eating. Not on purpose. I just lost my appetite. I couldn't eat. Then I miscarried. God, I had never seen so much blood." The elements of her story sounded familiar. The energetic pattern was the same: isolation and detachment in relationships, the total cessation of eating, and trauma related to her reproductive organs.

Jodi continued, "I felt so guilty. I starved my baby to death. Not on purpose. But I guess that's what happened. I got so depressed. My parents couldn't understand why. I was in such despair the rest of that year. That was my junior year and it was unbearable. I've had so much guilt for years and I've never told a soul."

"All that energy got stuck. Those feelings of loneliness and depression and guilt got stuck. They physically got stuck in your reproductive organs. They also got stuck in your relationship patterns and in the depths of your cellular memory, which can affect all aspects of your life and being," Carolanne explained. "Your bowel obstruction is trying to tell you that your shit is literally and symbolically stuck. Are you ready to shift it?"

"Yes, absolutely. Let's do it," Jodi responded immediately, eyes brightening. Then, done very simply and easily through the power of intention and breathwork, Carolanne witnessed a healing.

Three days later, Jodi called Carolanne to provide an update on her condition. "You are never going to believe what happened! I would have called sooner, but I've been on the toilet for the last three days, pretty much nonstop. Shitting my brains out. I'm not kidding. And if I'm not shitting, I'm eating. I've been ravenous. I've been eating like crazy. I don't think I've eaten like this since puberty. The energy is definitely moving again. Thank you so much."

"You did the work, Jodi. I'm just happy I could facilitate it and be a part of the healing." Although these post-session miracle update calls from clients that always began with "you're never going to believe what happened" were now routine, Carolanne never tired of receiving them. Witnessing miracles was the best part of her job.

Jodi continued, "Then this morning, when I woke up, my husband rolled over in bed and said 'we need to talk.' The first thing I noticed was that the big gray cloud hanging over his head was gone. It was the first meaningful conversation we have had in months. He told me that he was distant because he has been so scared by what's happening to me. He said he just didn't know how to express his fear or his feelings, that he was using anger as a way to avoid what was going on with me so he wouldn't have to feel the fear. He cried, and so did I. We both just got it all out."

"I am so happy to hear that. Isn't it amazing how your shift created the space for that conversation with your husband?" Carolanne was beaming. She loved these calls.

"Yeah, it's changed everything inside of me. Three days ago I would have said there was no hope for my marriage. Now I have hope. And joy.

And anticipation. I want to continue to clear my stuff and see what happens. When can I come back for another appointment?"

They looked at their schedules, but they just didn't sync up for the next four weeks. By this point, Carolanne knew not to force such things. There was always a reason. So Carolanne set Jodi's next appointment four weeks out.

Exactly four weeks later, Jodi showed up for her appointment with Carolanne. She was giddy, busting at the seams with excitement. Clearly, there was more good news.

"You're never going to believe what happened..." Jodi began.

"Try me," Carolanne teased.

"After our last conversation, I called my doctor. I asked her to do another test."

"Mm-hmm," Carolanne said. She loved to witness the radical reclamation of personal power.

"Yeah, after pooping my brains out and making up with my hubby, I just knew that my energy had shifted. If two of the three things we worked on in our session had shifted, I was sure that the cancer had, too. So, I just wanted to know for sure. You know, to shut up that nasty little skeptic that lives in my head."

"Uh-huh, it's always nice to get validation." Carolanne could relate. Despite being an energy healer and extremely into all things woo-woo herself, she was all too familiar with the vicious little skeptic who tried to take up residence in her ever-expanding mind.

"She didn't want to order the tests, of course. No surprise there. Especially because I told her that I was trying some alternative therapies. I could tell it took every ounce of her will not to roll her eyes at me then and there. But I didn't care. I was prepared to fight. I was insistent and told her I wasn't backing down and wanted the tests. Even if I had to fall down on the floor and have a temper tantrum. So, finally, she caved and I got my way," Jodi said matter-of-factly.

"And...?" Carolanne prompted, already knowing the answer but not wanting to miss the outward flowing of pure joy when Jodi expressed it.

"And guess what? No cancer! No sign of cancer at all! My doctors are baffled. They're calling it spontaneous remission. Spontaneous remission, my ass. That's transformation."

That, my friends, is power. And that kind of power can scale mountains. Every single one of you has access to that kind of power. Once you clear out your shit... er, stuck energy.

CELLULAR MEMORY–YOUR INFINITE STORAGE DATABASE

Your cellular memory–or DNA–holds all of the information that makes up the whole of you. This includes physical, mental, spiritual and emotional data. It's your blueprint. It's the energetic expression of the whole of your being. You may distinguish the different aspects of your being–mind, body, spirit–but the truth is that these are simply labels we have created as three-dimensional humans to try to grasp the bewildering nature of our multi-dimensional selves.

Your cellular memory is really a hologram. Each part of the hologram contains all of the information of the whole. This means you can access the entire blueprint for your whole multi-dimensional self in every single cell of your body. If anything is stuck, it's stuck in your cellular memory. Everything you've ever experienced is there. Everything your parents have ever experienced is there. Everything your ancestors experienced is there. If you're not happy with the state of your life, you can change it at the energetic source of your cellular memory hologram.

You are a powerful, magnificent being. And you have all the codes to heal and transform yourself. We just have a cool little technique that helps you to unlock them. It's so simple, so easy, and so accessible, with immediate results. Besides, you are worth it: worthy of infinite love, worthy of instant healing, and worthy of waking up to a new awareness of the brilliant, shining light that you are.

If you're human, you probably have some junk that muddies up your light. It's part of the human experience. The HEAL Technique® will help you to pinpoint when and where certain experiences muddied up your energy, and teaches you how to transform and transmute them, therefore transcending them. You are a powerhouse of energy. The tools in this book will help you to find where it's snagged up and stuck, and most importantly, will help you to unstick it. Imagine what you can do when you reclaim that kind of energy! Manifest your dreams and desires. Experience pure joy and passion in life. Heal yourself. Make miracles an everyday reality.

YOUR ORGANIC LIFE BLUEPRINT

A Course in Miracles[16] says miracles occur naturally, and when they are not occurring in your life, something has gone wrong. I like this idea. It means miracles are the norm, not the exception. It means we should expect them, every single day. It also means your life blueprint does not have to contain pain, suffering, trauma or drama.

Synchronicity, flow, effortless action and allowing... this is how life is supposed to be. Miracles. *This is your organic life blueprint.* The problem is, we often get in the way. Negative thinking, self-doubt, anxiety, fears, stuck energy and all of that other junk that's stuck in your cellular memory is getting in the way of allowing miracles to occur naturally. In order to move into a space in your life where you are living with the least amount of resistance possible, where you are creating your life in alignment with the truth of who you are that's deeply fulfilling–where miracles are part of the everyday–you have to deal with it (whatever it is) on an energetic level at the source.

WHEN ENERGY GETS STUCK

Ok, so we've already established that you are brilliantly and beautifully powerful beyond measure. I'll stop going on about this for a minute. Since you know this, why is it that you don't experience yourself as such all the time?

As humans, we all have a lot of emotional baggage: Unprocessed emotional events. Drama, drama, drama. What your mama did. What your daddy didn't do. Emotional scars. Out of whack emotional charges racked up from a range of childhood crap, both mundane and outlandish. Even if you have the best parents in the world and had a freaking fairytale childhood, your parents are still human. Stuck energy is part of the human experience. It's in your DNA. It gets passed down from ancestors, created in childhood, produced by our environment, accumulated from past lives, and a whole host of other things. The list goes on and on and on. Those emotional charges make you sluggish.

Get this: even positive emotional charges can get stuck. Yup, you heard me right. It isn't just the negative emotional charges that get stuck in our cellular memory. Even the highest of the highs can get stuck. Case in point: we all know of the middle-aged man with the beer belly and male pattern baldness who used to be the star quarterback. He drones on and on about his touchdowns and conquests, desperately hanging on to his high school glory days. That's stuck energy preventing him from moving forward in his life.

Your emotions are energy in motion that intuitively wants to move through your body. Flow is the natural state. Unfortunately, we interfere with the natural flow of emotions moving through us. We fear our emotions, or we deny, repress, or judge them. This impedes the natural flow of emotional energy within us.

Our bodies are a lot like computers. You've seen those desktops that are covered in icons with files everywhere. That mess slows your system down. It looks and feels like chaos, and it's nearly impossible to locate anything. This can feel overwhelming. We're all similar– when we fill all of our memory up with lots of intense, unprocessed emotional charges, it actually slows our system down. This impacts our performance and capacity, but we can upgrade our system and neutralize those charges, to clear up some space for energy to flow.

You see, it's about getting back to neutral. When you allow energy to flow in one direction and not the other, it gets stuck. When you bring the two sides together, this creates balance, and it creates flow. We live in a polarized universe of duality: Positive and negative. Good and bad. Light and dark. Masculine and feminine. Energy is created when you bring the two polarities together. Just like a battery, you need both the positive and negative polarities to come together in order to generate energy. To create life, you need both the male and the female. All of creation requires energy. Disease is an imbalance of energy. Not being able to manifest the life of your dreams is an imbalance of energy. When miracles don't occur naturally, you can be sure there's an imbalance of energy. When you have an imbalance of energy, you have limitation. Your thinking is limited. When your thinking is limited, this limits your ability to see opportunities. When you can't see opportunities, your experience becomes limited. You're essentially running around in circles in a pattern of limitation, doing the same thing over and over again but expecting a different result. Strengthening the neural pathways of limitation in your brain reinforces a program and pattern of limitation in the experience of your life. You believe in limitation because you're wired to, then you experience limitation and it reinforces your belief, keeping you locked up in that very pattern of limitation.

WHAT'S THE SOURCE OF THE IMBALANCE?

The first thing we determine using the HEAL Technique® is where the original source of the emotional blockage comes from. We often think we are the birthplace of the blockage, and that is sometimes true. But not always.

YOU

If the emotional charge that is locked inside your own cellular memory is from an event that you experienced at some point from birth until the present, then it's yours. If it's in your cellular memory from something you experienced in the womb before birth, it's yours. If it's from your own personal past life and you carried it with your spirit into this incarnation, it's still yours.

It comes from a decision you made, most often an unconscious decision. This could look like Jodi's story of cervical cancer and bowel obstruction caused by her energetic pattern of depression, shame and guilt. It might be unresolved childhood emotional trauma caused by an abusive alcoholic father who showered you with attention and gifts because he felt bad after drinking binges, which manifests today as a pattern of attracting men who are alcoholic and abusive. This could even look like anxiety and claustrophobia because you were suffocated in a past life. Either way, it's yours. It originated with your soul in this life or a previous one. These are a piece of cake to clear. The HEAL Technique® helps you to awaken the energetic blocks that are stuck in the subconscious mind, and allows them to rise into your conscious awareness so that you can clear it.

SOMEONE ELSE

Your own snagged-up energy may not be the only thing that is blocking you from experiencing the fullest expression of your authentic self. When we get to the source of the energetic block, sometimes you will find that it's not yours.

We are energetic beings. Our brains and bodies are like big radio antennae, exchanging information with the energies of others all the time, whether we are aware of it or not. Sometimes the source of your energetic block is not you at all. You are simply "picking up" on the energy of the people closest to you–your husband or wife, boyfriend or girlfriend, parents, children, or other family and friends–and your body has made the decision to take it on as your own.

Sometimes the "someone else" is an ancestor and you have inherited their emotional or energetic patterns through your genetic memory. Genetic memory is a memory present at birth that is just there, with no sensory experience to explain why it's there. Scientists think genetic memory is incorporated into the genetic code over time. Brian G. Dias and Kerry J. Ressler published an article in *Nature Neuroscience* describing studies of mice that have indicated the experiences of one generation can influence the behavior and brains of later generations. Mice trained to fear and avoid a particular smell passed their aversion and fear of the same smell to subsequent generations, even though they had never encountered it or been trained to fear it.[17]

Unresolved emotions and traumas experienced by an ancestor may be creating obstacles for you today and blocking your path towards manifesting everything you want to create in your life. Clearing this stuck energy from someone else–whether you are picking up on the frequency of those close to you or have inherited it through your genetics–can be cleared the same way. The HEAL Technique® can help you to transform the energetic patterns that you are living out that are not in your highest good, and free you from the energetic cords or patterns that are not serving you. When you shift, everyone around you shifts.

Where it really gets tricky is when *you are your ancestor*. Your blockage shows up as being both yours and someone else's. What that typically means is that in addition to being gifted your funky pattern through your ancestral DNA, you have also carried it through your own personal consciousness from prior lives. As if you were your great-great-grandmother, you'd have the energetic blocks and unresolved emotions of that particular lifetime passed down to you through your genetic inheritance, plus the cellular memory of that past life event. Lucky you.

Carolanne has had her own personal–and validated–experience with this. For as long as she can remember, she's had restless legs syndrome (RLS). RLS is a disorder of the nervous systems that affects the legs and causes an uncontrollable urge to move them. Symptoms typically occur at night, so it can impact sleep. The causes of RLS are unknown.[18] RLS is known to run in families, and Carolanne's brother suffers from it, too. Sometimes her RLS is so severe that she can't sleep at night at all. One night, in the midst of frustration at two o'clock in the morning, she realized that she could use her own HEAL Technique® to rid herself of this silly RLS suffering. Without getting out of bed, she did a quick session on herself.

It may sound complicated right now, but I promise: it's super easy. You'll learn how to do all of this by the end of this book. But pay attention to the process. Get a feel for it. Put yourself in the stories so you can try it on for size. That way, when you get to the work of clearing up your own stuff, you will have had a few practice runs and the technique will seem more familiar.

Carolanne began by calibrating her starting vibration in reference to being free of RLS. She uncovered that she was vibrating at a frequency of zero and ninety, which corresponds to fear and rage. These were not normal emotions for her. Next, she tested herself to find the source.

"Is it mine?" she asked her body and tested. *No*, her body revealed.

"It is someone else?" she asked. *Yes*, her body answered.

"Is it something else?" she asked. *No.*

So it was someone else. But who? She would ask her body to reveal that in a minute. First she had to find the brainwave state.

What brainwave state is this in? Carolanne asked her body.

Beta and theta, her body revealed. Physical and mental.

Next, she tuned in to her own emotions about the situation. She put her hand on her heart and turned her focus inward. *How does it make me feel when I have RLS?* she asked herself silently.

Angry. Getting up at night to take hot baths in the hope that she could settle her legs was insufferable. She hated taking herbs or medicines to help her sleep because she couldn't stand feeling groggy the next day.

Carolanne then felt into the emotions of the anger, asking herself, *how does it feel when I am angry?*

She immediately felt her teeth clench. She felt anxious. Then Carolanne felt into her anxiety and asked herself without a sound, *what's underneath these feelings of anxiety?*

Helplessness. *What if I never get rid of it?* she worried. Under the feeling of helplessness, she found feelings of fear, sadness and despair. They were hiding out in the shadows.

She closed her eyes and felt into the energy of these emotions. She wanted to find the source. Where in her ancestral line did these feelings begin? She asked her body to reveal a number. The number four popped into her head. So the source was an ancestor four generations back.

She tuned in again to feel into the energy. Was it male or female? She could sense masculine energy, so she knew it was male.

Is it mom's side or dad's side? she asked. *Mom's,* she discovered, because her mom's face appeared in her mind's eye.

Is it mom's mom or mom's dad? she asked. *Mom's dad,* she got as an answer.

Is it his dad or his mom? she wondered. *His grandfather,* her subconscious revealed.

So, it was her grandfather's grandfather on her mom's side. *Interesting,* she thought.

She felt into the feelings of anger, anxiety, helplessness, fear, sadness and despair. *Show me more,* she asked herself silently. *Why would you feel these things? What triggered it?* Then she pretended that she could connect with this ancestor so that he could reveal his story.

He was angry and full of despair because he lost someone he loved. A child. He wished he could have done something to prevent it. There was so much pain and sadness. Suddenly, Carolanne felt a throbbing and pulling in her legs and the overwhelming urge to bounce them up and down. She was overcome by a deep restlessness driven by feelings of regret. She turned her attention inward again and asked her ancestor quietly if he would like her to do a healing. Immediately, she imagined that he answered with a resounding *yes!*

She drew in a long, deep breath and centered herself in her heart. In her imagination, she pretended to grab both of his hands and told him to let go of all the feelings of despair, fear, sadness, anxiety and anger. *I'm your great-great-granddaughter. Did you know that all of these emotions got locked into our DNA and are affecting me on a physical level today?* she asked him.

No, he answered sadly.

Would you like to let it all go, and free your future generations from this pattern of emotions? she asked.

Yes, he answered solemnly.

She wanted to know in her own heart what the benefit of this experience had been. With her hands placed on her heart, she posed that question to herself.

Then she understood: *The best benefit is knowing that I can heal myself. That I am aware, empowered, validated, light and free.*

Out loud, she set the intent to free him of his pain. To surrender the feelings of anger, anxiety, helplessness, fear, sadness and despair. By doing so, she would free herself and anyone else in her genetic lineage who had this pattern of emotion encoded in her DNA.

At the beginning of her impromptu session in bed, Carolanne found that this pattern was stuck in the beta and theta brainwaves. She progressed through the corresponding breath work, beginning with nose-mouth breaths for theta. Thirteen of them. Twelve in the nose, filling her lungs completely, delivering oxygen throughout her system to gather up the stuck energy. Twelve breaths pushed out of the mouth–a complete cycle– clearing the pattern on the mental level in the theta brainwave state. On the thirteenth intake of air she held her breath, swallowing the oxygen down, marinating in it– a doorway to a new level of consciousness.

Next, she moved on to the mouth-mouth breaths for the beta brainwave state. She drew in deep, exaggerated, full breaths through her mouth, the air making a hissing sound as it passed through her teeth. She pushed out full, complete breaths from her lungs, her lips forming an "o" like when you say "ooh." She breathed in and out through her mouth twelve times, air audibly whooshing in and out, cleansing and clearing the patterns that had been locked away in her DNA for four generations– a completed cycle of experience. She held the thirteenth breath for as long as she could, allowing the oxygen to infuse her healing as she swallowed that last breath down into her belly. When she couldn't hold it any longer, she blew it out of her mouth with a huge sigh.

She sat still with her eyes closed, high from the immense oxygenation flowing through her. She allowed the dizzies to work through her, clearing her of the pattern of energy that made her legs restless. She could feel that the thirteenth breath was the doorway to the next level in the spiral of life. The pattern was clear.

When she felt grounded again, she opened her eyes and felt a heart full of gratitude. Then, she yawned an enormous yawn and knew her vibration had shifted. Her legs were calm. Her heart was calm. She let out another long, drawn out yawn and fell fast asleep.

In the morning, self-doubt set in. Carolanne told herself that she had made the whole thing up in her imagination and that the only reason she fell asleep was because she had finally been tired enough to sleep. The real test would be lying down to go to sleep that night. Would RLS be an unwelcome guest in her bed again?

When she instantaneously fell asleep that second night, Carolanne became curious. She called her mom to ask questions about her family history. While dialing the phone, she made a commitment to herself that it didn't matter if she had made it up or not. Even if it was all pretend, it had worked. It changed the energy for her and she was able to sleep soundly for two nights in a row. This was not typical for her, and was a welcome relief.

"Hello?" Carolanne's mom answered the phone.

Carolanne told her what she discovered through her self-healing session, sharing what she had learned about her great-great-grandfather. Then she asked her mom, "Do you know if someone on Grandpa Chick's side lost a child?"

"Carolanne, back in those days, it was common for kids to die for all kinds of reasons. I don't know of any specific story about my great-grandfather, but why don't you log in to Ancestry.com and see what you can find."

As soon as Carolanne was off the phone, she grabbed her iPad to begin investigating. Before she could even log in to Ancestry.com, she noticed an email notification from the site. It was alerting her that someone in her family had updated their family tree. That really piqued her interest. She logged in and found that her family tree had 2045 connections! She immediately focused in on her mom's side of the tree and followed the connection four generations back: first to her mom's dad, Carolanne's Grandpa Chick, and then back two more generations to his grandfather. His name was John McCarty.

Weird, that's my brother's name, Carolanne thought to herself. She found that ironic, especially since her brother John suffered from RLS.

Carolanne learned that her great-great-grandfather, John McCarty, lost his firstborn son, Claude, who was born in 1879. He died in 1890 at the age of eleven. Chills tingled her spine, goosebumps visibly popped up on her arms and she shivered.

Coincidence? I think not.

SOMETHING ELSE

Sometimes, as was referenced during Carolanne's impromptu healing session, your energy gets stuck and it's simply not yours or someone else's. It's *something* else. This is where it gets a little freaky. Something else could be anything else. Literally, ANYTHING else that informs your blueprint that is not an organic part of your authentic self. It could be your environment, the media, or the food you eat. It could be your cultural programming or the pervading social narrative of the consumer culture. It could even be other energies. It doesn't matter what it is, if it affects you it's now your responsibility to clear it. If a neighbor's dog poops in your front yard and you don't want to step in shit when you come home from work, you're going to want to clean up the nasty. Same-same.

Believe it or not, this freaky thing happened to me. I went to Carolanne for a HEAL session because I found myself eating compulsively. This was happening *constantly* and I was gaining weight as a result. It came on very suddenly and persisted for two weeks. It absolutely baffled me. I would start every day with the intention to eat healthy foods that would help me to shed the weight. I vowed only to eat when I was hungry and to stop when I was full. This had always worked for me in the past, but this time was different somehow. I felt hungry and anxious and the only thing that soothed me was eating. I'm not talking about eating a small healthy snack. I was craving–and devouring–foods that I would never normally touch. You see, I'm a health nut. I eat a mostly raw vegetarian diet and can be a bit fanatical about nourishing myself with organic whole foods. I rarely touch processed food. But what I was craving were things I wouldn't even call food in my normal life, like Oreos with milk, potato chips and soda. It made no sense and I didn't know what had suddenly happened to me. It wasn't just the unhealthy food cravings that perplexed me, either. It was the feelings of anxiety, nervousness and restlessness I felt when I wasn't bingeing, the frenzy I felt when I was, and the shame, guilt and emptiness I felt after.

In the session, we uncovered that the energy was not mine. It was something else. Using her intuition—by pretending—Carolanne told me that there was a female spirit attached to me who had recently passed and was on my father's side of the family. She described an incredibly sad woman who did not realize she had died. Carolanne felt that the woman died of a broken heart. What I had not told Carolanne until she revealed this to me was that just a few weeks before, my dad's cousin's daughter Janet passed away very unexpectedly in her sleep at her parents' home, at the age of thirty-five. The cause of death was not yet known, at least not by my dad or me. She was morbidly obese and had lost her husband to cancer not too long before her own death. She had been depressed and her parents were worried about her, so she had moved back in with them as she mourned the loss of her husband.

Carolanne guided me to clear her energy. We went outside in the Florida sunshine and put our bare feet in the earth. I closed my eyes and centered myself with a few deep breaths. I used my imagination to pretend that Janet was there. In my mind's eye, with Carolanne's guidance, I led Janet into an elevator that went through a portal into the center of the Earth. In my imagination, it was like Willy Wonka's great glass elevator. From the center of the Earth, we shot towards the center of the sun with the help of the magical glass elevator. Once I saw the sun, I suddenly understood why people who have near death experiences sometimes see a tunnel and a bright light. *This must be where they go*, I thought to myself, marveling at my imagination. Carolanne guided me to take Janet to the light and to help her to cross over with the energy of love. It was quick, painless, and quite easy. Who knows if it was real or not. It doesn't matter. After that, the cravings and bingeing ended and my body found its natural balance pretty easily. So, I got the result I was looking for.

WHAT IS YOUR STUCK ENERGY SITUATION TRYING TO TELL YOU?

Stuck energy could be triggered by little things like the time you tripped in middle school and the cool kids all laughed at you, to the big things like death, childbirth, illness, miscarriage or other equally serious shit. It may look like unworthiness, the inability to receive, lack of self-love, feeling like you're not enough, self-sabotage, fear, feeling stuck, attracting the same losers into your life over and over again, negative thinking, anxiety, depression, insomnia, excess weight, eating disorders, addictions, or physical disease. It's all just stuck emotion or a pattern of emotions in the subconscious that pops in from time to time, pretending to screw up your life. But that's just a masquerade. It's really a call to something greater: A call to find the greater truth about yourself. A call to live a greater truth in your life, to become the fullest expression of yourself. Who do you think programmed these events anyway? Your higher self already orchestrated your journey of destiny. Your higher self has guided you with every breath. Trust that there has been a purpose to your pain and suffering. This is where compassionate self-love can happen. The butterfly that flies the highest must first build the strongest cocoon. Pain is your cocoon and you are getting ready for flight.

Sometimes energy just gets stuck. The reasons for it are vast and varied. Infinite, probably. Emotions are simply energy in motion. All charged emotions, if left unresolved, sit in a trauma state. That's stuck energy. Blocked. Immobile. Stagnant. Stuck energy manifests in many different ways and often manifests progressively, gradually getting more and more extreme with each manifestation.

Shamanic traditions have understood for centuries that the luminous energy field that surrounds the body is encoded with information. It contains the blueprint for life. The information in this blueprint informs and organizes the physical body. Shamanic traditions recognize that the information in this energy field is the cause of illness and disease, and that the genetic blueprint is energetic at its source. This energy field is what informs the DNA, which then informs the physical body. This energy field becomes toxic when we experience highly charged emotions that we cannot process effectively. Trauma reorganizes the energy that informs the blueprint. If it has a charge that was not released in the moment, it imbeds itself into our energetic field and imprints there. True healing involves clearing the imprint in the field so that it can re-inform the field, which in turn re-informs the universe. If we do not heal and clear it, energy becomes stuck. That stuck energy shows up as unhealthy patterns in our lives.

Stuck energy sucks. That's not a euphemism. It really sucks. It sucks you dry of your life force. It becomes a feeding frenzy of energy that is feeding upon itself, cannibalizing each area of your life until you unstick it and allow it to flow again. When you have stagnant energy, you're limited. Your thinking is limited, you have limited perspective and your life is limited. When you're limited, the limitation prevents you from experiencing your authentic power and the full truth of who you are. It keeps you in a holding pattern of being stuck in the same rut. You CANNOT and WILL NOT achieve a new result with the same old-same old. That's the definition of insanity, anyway. You need a new process to get a new result.

Your emotions are energy *in motion*. That means they naturally want to move through your being. The problem is, we get in the way. We don't allow the energy to move. We don't allow the flow of emotions. We stuff them. We avoid them. We numb to them. We judge them. We judge ourselves for having them. We judge ourselves for avoiding them. We judge ourselves for numbing them. We judge ourselves for judging them. All of this shuts down the energetic flow.

Your bio-energetic field–that nifty donut-shaped electromagnetic field around your body that contains the blueprint for your life–becomes toxic when energy gets stuck, which then reorganizes the energy that is informing your blueprint. Your electromagnetic blueprint is informing the greater energy field around you.

There is a constant breathing in and out of energy going on in the body. Your toroidal energy field is electromagnetic, too. The "electro" is the frequency you are putting out, informing the universe around you. The "magnetic" is what you are pulling back in, what is magnetizing towards you as the universe responds in kind. What this means is that your energetic field is choreographing life experiences to recreate the circumstances of the original wounding in order to give you the opportunity to heal. If you do not heal the energetic source of that original wound, you get stuck in a pattern of recreating the same events until you are able to heal it and clear it at the energetic source. You know that same loser that you kept dating over and over again? Same relationship, ten different men. Or that dead end job and ungrateful boss you kept bouncing to from workplace to workplace? Yeah, that's the pattern I'm talking about.

The intention of this book is to guide you through a process of shifting stuck energy, and breaking free from the patterns that limit you. We'll dive straight to the source of the energetic block and clear the stagnant energy lodged and festering inside of you, clearing a pathway for energy to flow freely again. We'll look at when and where your energies got snagged up and stuck. We'll uncover your personal energetic patterns of belief and examine the belief systems that keep you stuck. Then we'll find your personal healing codes to unlock and release yourself from the repeating pattern of stuck energy. With those unique codes, we'll know exactly how to go in and neutralize the charges to free up the stuck energy and obliterate the energetic block. This allows energy to flow. When energy flows, new doors open. When energy flows, new neural pathways are built in the brain. When energy flows, you open channels in your brain that allow new information to stream in effortlessly. This brings new awareness, new perspective, new insights, new opportunities, *a new paradigm.*

It's the simplest shift in your energetic vibration, but it can radically transform your entire life.

Today, we know that our DNA holds the blueprint for the complete design of our physical bodies. Our DNA also holds the plan for the emotional, mental and spiritual aspects of ourselves. Cellular memory is the complete blueprint for your entire existence.

Our bodies are made up of billions of cells that are always in a state of flux: transformation, death and renewal. Through it all, the cell has a memory from this life, from our previous lifetimes, and from our ancestors. Every experience we have ever had in this lifetime or in previous lives, or any experience inherited from our genetic heritage, is contained within our cells. Much of it is hidden away from our conscious minds. That's how our DNA is programmed. Almost all of it is subconscious or unconscious.

If you're not happy with the program you've inherited (and let's face it, who really is?) you have the power to change it, and to reprogram yourself. As we grow, evolve and transform any aspect of ourselves or of our lives, our cells are constantly updating our personal data. As we shift vibrations, we can re-inform the blueprint. Higher, faster vibrations cannot coexist with lower, slower ones. Once the blueprint is re-informed and reorganizes along a new vibration, it can no longer hold the old pattern in place. That has a ripple effect that touches all aspects of your life, for all of the people connected to you and for generations to come.

4) YOU ARE PURE POTENTIAL: *Balancing Your Energy*

Energetically, you're huge. You're a whole universe. In your most essential state, you are pure consciousness, an entire universe of pure potential and possibility. In order to fit all that awesomeness into your comparatively tiny human body, your soul had to experience compression and limitation. Huge limitation. Otherwise, you just wouldn't fit.

The whole you, the real you, is so much more. You have a body. You have a mind. You have a spirit. The operative word here: ***have***. You are not your body, or your mind, or your spirit. You are the one who *has* all of these things, as a vehicle of experience, expression and information. You are not your body, you are the being who inhabits your body. You are not your thoughts, you are the being behind your thoughts. You are not even your spirit. You are the culmination of all of these things and more. You are greater than the sum of all of your parts. You are an entire universe.

BALANCING YOUR ENERGY

You're an entire universe of energy. In order for all that energy to take up residence in your physical body, it had to condense. Before you moved into that clever body of yours, you were pure consciousness, a spark of divinity. That's how all matter forms: a spark.

In order for energy to become matter, it all begins with a spark: a spark of consciousness. Something has to invoke it. That spark begins with the perfect balance of two energies coming together. When you bring two energies together, there's a spark that creates energy, vibration and momentum.

Everything in nature has both positive and negative polarities, including us. When the positive and negative aspects of ourselves are in balance, we have power. Think of a battery. It takes both the positive and negative polarity to power the battery. Balancing the two polarities is what generates the energy. We are no different.

Everything in nature seeks balance, and you are part of nature. Your being seeks balance. Balance is neutrality: Balancing the positive and negative emotional charges. Balancing the light and dark in our being. Balancing the yin and the yang. Think of yin and yang as complementary opposing forces. When they come together in balance, they form a whole. The balanced whole is greater than the sum of its parts. The power is in finding the balance point.

Here's the thing about energy: energy is just energy. It doesn't care if it has a positive charge or a negative charge. Energy doesn't care what label you give it. Energy doesn't care what you believe. Energy doesn't care if the ego labels it right or wrong, good or bad. Sometimes even supercharged positive experiences can take us out of balance as much as the negative ones can, on a cellular level. We tend to think negative traumatic events are the only things that shift our energy out of balance. The truth is that both positive and negative experiences can pull your energy out of balance. Getting married, the birth of a baby, the start of your new dream job, an exciting new move– these are all wonderful events that have the potential to create a charge and knock your energy off balance. You remember the balding forty-something with the beer belly who sits at the bar reminiscing about his high school glory days as the star quarterback, who would have gone pro if only he hadn't had that devastating knee injury? Think about it. It isn't the negative event of the knee injury that keeps him stuck; it's the super high charge of energy around being the star quarterback that prevents him from moving forward.

All disease is brought about by a lack of energy. Anything in your life that you want to heal or change is there due to a lack of energy. If you've been unable to create or manifest a desire, it's because of a lack of energy. Whatever is blocking you from living to your highest potential is this same lack of energy.

Remember, energy is created when you bring the two polarities together. You need both the positive and negative polarities to come together in order to produce energy. This balance of polarities generates energy. Neutralizing the charges–both positive and negative–opens up the energy so it can flow again. Bringing yourself back into balance is what gives you the upwelling of energy needed to heal from disease, manifest your dreams, attract your desires, express your potential, find your purpose, and live your highest potential.

You came into this world with a plan, a path, a purpose. You're going to experience certain things on your path. You are going to go through your plan one way or another. It's mapped out for you as part of your blueprint. You can go through your plan with struggle and resistance, or with amazing empowerment. It's up to you how you choose to experience it. You can experience it from a high vibration or a low one. This chapter discusses the patterns that get in your way and cause you to resist your true path, creating struggle and suffering. You will also learn how to ready yourself for your organic life path so that you can be who you came here to be and do what you came here to do, experiencing your path from the highest vibration possible.

The HEAL Technique® work is about balancing these polarities and generating the energy so that it flows freely through your being. It is about neutralizing the charges of unprocessed emotions so that you can free the deep-rooted, dormant energy and allow renewed energy to create something new in your life. This is true freedom: Freedom from the old, stagnant energy. Freedom from old patterns that don't serve you. When you balance yourself, you become free to be one hundred percent of who you really are. You become free to live authentically. You become free to bring the truth of who you are to the world. And that, my friend, is a *gift*.

FULL SPECTRUM HEALING

You've heard of broad-spectrum antibiotics. They're antibiotics specially designed to fight against a wide range of disease-causing microorganisms. They're great if a patient needs to be cured quickly of an infection. They are really handy if the doctor can't diagnose the exact strain of bacteria causing the illness.

The HEAL Technique® is like that. It's a broad-spectrum healing technique that was specifically designed to neutralize and heal the full range of energetic causes. It's great if you want an instant healing, and really handy when you don't want to get into the drama of the story that caused it. It's the best technique when you just want it gone, on all levels and in all combinations. You're a full spectrum being, and the HEAL Technique® addresses full spectrum healing, bringing your whole, awesome, multi-dimensional self back into happy balance.

It really is as simple as getting into your heart. Think of your heart as the neutral zone. Living from your heart enables you to pull the higher self in to experience the physical self. The heart is the doorway to the divine. It's the key to experiencing heaven here and now.

5) YOU ARE HEART-CENTERED: *Living From Your Heart*

BODY FULL OF SOUL

Her husband had become a stranger to her. She didn't even know who he was anymore. Granted, she had been sick for a long, long time. Most of her energy had been focused on her healing and recovery or on raising their two young children, and they had steadily been growing more and more distant over the last five years. Her spiritual awakening only expanded the gulf between them. Carolanne was no longer the woman her husband had married. She really had changed quite dramatically. She had no intention of ever going back to what she was before. How could she? She was just beginning to come into her power. She had finally found her purpose and was on her life path. She realized that she was as much of a stranger to him as he was to her.

Joey hated watching Carolanne suffer with her illness. Illness had taken his wife away from him. It wasn't too long ago that they were making plans for their young children because death was looming and he was powerless to stop it. Joey felt hopeless. Despair occupied him, filling him up completely. Any place where despair wasn't already permeating his being, fear paralyzed him instead. He didn't know how to express his feelings. He was too ashamed to burden Carolanne with his anguish anyway, so he stuffed them, or numbed them. When he stuffed his feelings, they always found ways to sneak out and boil over as distorted expressions of ego. What started out as hopelessness and despair stormed out guns a-blazing as anger and sarcasm. A lot of sarcasm. When he became numb to his feelings, he binged on food or alcohol or spent money. Lots of money, at a time when they were under huge financial strain because he was not working and they were living off of Carolanne's disability checks.

Even more than the illness, Joey felt that Carolanne's healing and subsequent awakening took her even further away from him. She had found something enormously profound and mysterious. He felt abandoned, like she didn't need him anymore. Joey felt threatened, a little bit jealous, and deeply, deeply resentful. Whatever it was that she had found truly disrupted his belief system.

Ashamed and despondent, Joey stuffed and numbed his feelings. He lost hope. *He lost heart.* As he lost himself, his behavior grew more erratic and irresponsible... and hugely destructive to their marriage. He became more and more of a recluse. He retreated into himself. Carolanne felt alone, abandoned, betrayed and devastated. She had had enough.

It was time to talk. Time to be honest, and definitely time for something to shift. Her marriage was on its last whimper. There was no landmark event that provided the driving force to finally discuss ending their relationship, just a general pervading sense of exhaustion and sorrow. So she knocked back a couple glasses of wine to summon the courage to tell him it was over.

One Friday night, after she tucked her kids into bed, she knew it was time. Carolanne and Joey sat down on their back porch and she told him it was over. He told her that he would do whatever he had to in order to win her back. She didn't say anything but thought furtively, *Good luck, buddy. Not happening.* She was done. Besides, all of her programming and conditioning told her that there was no way that she could make their marriage work, even if she wanted it to, after all the shit he had pulled.

At the end of the evening, they agreed it was the end of their marriage. Together, they decided it would be best to move on quickly. Their relationship was toxic and the family was suffering. That night, they moved through the home they had built together and very matter-of-factly divvied up their belongings. *You take this, I'll keep that.* Their many years together had been reduced to a divided household inventory on wide-ruled paper, torn from their daughter's school notebook.

The next day, the kids were scheduled to go to a sleepover birthday party. They committed to telling the kids the news on Sunday after they came home from the party. They wanted to allow their children to enjoy the weekend without heartache, tears and worry. Besides, four weeks prior Carolanne had already committed to attending an indigenous healing ceremony that Saturday night. She was going to check it out for one of her clients, but she knew she could use a healing, too.

After lunch on Saturday, Joey took their children to the sleepover party. As soon as the house was silent and she was alone, it hit her. A pair of thugs–Despair and Grief–punched Carolanne in the gut. They knocked the wind out of her. Her body went limp and she fell to the kitchen floor. She had a full-fledged, out-and-out breakdown. It was the most emotionally intense moment of her life. The pain and anguish bubbled up from deep within and escaped in tones of sorrow and mourning. Sobbing came from unfathomable depths within the core of her being that she didn't even know existed. Her body convulsed in a pile on the kitchen floor as she wept and wept. The sounds that escaped her lips were haunting even to her own ears.

Just then, Joey walked into the kitchen. She didn't even hear him come home, she was so absorbed in her agony and bawling. He rushed over to his wife, a heap of emotion on the floor, and took her into his arms. Then he just lost it. Tears streamed down his face and sobs wracked his body. He just wanted to end her pain. He loathed himself for being the cause of it.

"You have to get up and go get a healing," he said, begging her to go to the indigenous healing ceremony. Not for her client, but for herself.

She couldn't answer. She could only weep.

"Please… you need a healing…" He was desperate. Pleading.

Still no answer from Carolanne, just silent sobbing. Her energy was waning.

"Go get a healing. You need a healing. Go get a healing. You need a healing. Please. Please. Please. Please. Please. Go get a healing. You need a healing…" He recited his plea like an insane and desperate mantra. It was surreal. It was lunacy. And it frightened her a little.

Without another word, Carolanne pulled herself up. She unwadded the damp, soggy tissue in her hands and blew her nose so she could breathe. She dabbed her sore swollen eyes and took a long deep breath. She held her breath for just a pause, then exhaled entirely. After a few more breaths like this, she picked up the phone and called the shaman. Carolanne described the circumstances of her afternoon as best she could, her voice still shaky.

"Should I still come?" she wondered aloud.

"Please come," the shaman invited her. "You need a healing."

Carolanne splashed her face with cold water, put on a pair of oversized dark sunglasses and headed out the door. When she arrived at the yoga studio about twenty minutes later, she felt more centered. Emotionally spent, but centered and calm.

She was so grateful that the lights in the studio were dim. From what she could see through her puffy bloodshot eyes, there were about twenty people in the space and they were ready to begin. *Thank goodness I don't have to make small talk or face anybody,* she thought gratefully.

Carolanne took her place in the healing circle and settled in. This particular indigenous healing ceremony required participants to sit in silence for several hours and go within. It was an opportunity to receive healing from a skilled shaman as well as an opportunity to take part in her own healing. Holding her own healing intention in her heart, Carolanne went inside.

After sitting in silence for about an hour, Carolanne unexpectedly had a vision. She was standing in a cemetery, holding hands with her children. Little Joey was holding her right hand, Sonoma holding her left. They were holding hands so tightly that their knuckles were white and her fingers were numb. The vision seemed so real because she could feel the sweat and moisture in her hands as she gripped the hands of her children. They watched together as her husband's coffin was being lowered into the ground.

The vision replayed over and over again like a hellish nightmare on a loop. Over and over again she clutched her children's hands. Over and over again she witnessed her husband's coffin being lowered into the earth. Each time she saw his coffin settle into the dirt, she thought the nightmare would end. Each time it started over again, forcing her to observe the wretched, heartbreaking scene again.

Finally, she screamed in her vision, "Enough! Is there anything I can do to change it?"

Just then, she heard a small, sputtering aircraft overhead. She looked up and for the first time noticed the clear, still, blue sky. Not a cloud in sight. Her grip on her children's hands relaxed slightly. She allowed herself to breathe. The airplane started maneuvering through the sky. It was a skywriter! Meticulously, the plane wrote out the word "yes" in fluffy white smoke letters as tall as the Empire State Building. The message must have stretched on for many miles.

"What can I do?" Carolanne asked. Just then, the plane flew towards the bright beaming sun. Carolanne's gaze followed the aircraft. She blinked her eyes at the intensely bright light. Then she found her consciousness transported instantaneously to the center of the sun. When she opened her eyes again, what she saw was beyond description. It was breathtaking.

She drew in a slow, lingering inhale of breath and tried to take it all in. That's when she saw him standing there. It was Joey. She ran over and embraced him.

"What is going on? What are you doing here?" she asked. She was confused and scared and wanted answers, pronto.

"This is my place. I like it here. And I am never going back there." He cast his eyes down in disgust towards Earth.

"If you're here, then *who is that*?" Carolanne demanded, spitting out her words. If Joey's essence was here in this place, who was there masquerading as her husband?

"Oh, that guy. No one, really. He's just running programs," Joey answered very pragmatically.

"What? What do you mean?" She was so baffled and confused.

"There's no soul in him. He's just running programs," the real Joey responded.

"What do you mean by 'programs'?" Carolanne persisted.

"He's on autopilot," Joey explained.

"How do we get you back there?" Carolanne asked. She was starting to feel desperation creep in.

"I am not going back there. No way. I've already ruined everything." He was somber.

49

"What's going to happen?" Carolanne's curiosity took over. She never entertained the possibility that her husband had literally checked out. It made sense. It resonated. She certainly felt like his soul had checked out.

"Well, autopilot can only run for so long, then the programs shut down. It sort of... self destructs," Joey responded honestly. That made sense to Carolanne, too. She thought he was on a path of self-destruction. And here was his soul, confirming what she knew to be true.

"What runs the programs?" Carolanne asked. She was in investigator mode. If she was going to transform her marriage, she would have to understand what was really going on, and heal it at its source.

"The ego," he revealed.

"You're coming back with me," Carolanne declared. She was prepared to get forceful in order to get her husband back.

"No, I'm not," he insisted.

She had just spent five hours watching him get buried over and over again. She was ready to get to the good part, and she knew this was it. But before she could make her demands, the ceremony was over. The music stopped. The shaman was closing the healing circle with a rite of protection. Carolanne squeezed her eyes tightly again, trying to go back in. But it was gone. She was back in the shadowy yoga studio. She didn't know where her husband actually was, but she knew for sure that he was not in his body. "What do I do now?" she asked before she opened her eyes.

Then, she heard a voice. It sounded a lot like her own voice, but more relaxed and sure of herself. "*Wait for my instructions,*" said the voice enigmatically.

As soon as she said her goodbyes, Carolanne headed home. She was relieved to find Joey's car in the driveway. When she went into the house, she saw him sleeping on the sofa. She was grateful that he was home, but she was also still seething with anger at him. She could feel a fire boiling in her belly.

Carolanne walked out onto the back patio to take in some fresh air. She wanted to center herself before going to bed. After a couple of deep breaths and a few moments of silence, Carolanne heard the voice again. "*Go inside and put your hand on his heart,*" it said.

Obediently, she went back inside the house. But the sight of him snoring on the sofa bubbled up the fury in her belly again. *Fuck that*, she thought. *He doesn't deserve my touch.* So she went to her room and went to bed without a second thought.

About twenty minutes after she fell asleep, she heard the voice again. "*Get up,*" the voice demanded.

Carolanne didn't want to.

"*Get up.*" The voice was getting bossy.

Carolanne didn't budge.

"*Get up,*" the voice insisted. Carolanne knew this would only continue, so she reluctantly flung off the covers, got out of bed and went in search of Joey.

He was nowhere in sight. Terror immediately settled in her chest. She remembered the nightmarish replay of her vision in the cemetery. She was terrified that she would find him dead. Is that what the voice wanted?

She peeked outside. His car was still there. She proceeded to go through the house room by room, thinking to herself, *If I find him dead because I went to sleep without listening to that damn voice, I will never forgive myself.*

Opening her daughter's bedroom door, relief washed over her body. She let out a gasp of air, grateful to find her husband alive. He was lying there in Sonoma's bed. His eyes fluttered open when he heard Carolanne sigh. She saw the same terror in his eyes that she felt inside. When their eyes connected, they both started to cry. She wasn't sure if she was crying now because she was just a few hours from telling the kids that they were splitting up, or if she was sad about losing her husband, or because she was afraid that he would hurt himself. It was probably a combination of all of these things, and more.

Carolanne drew a deep breath in and gathered up as much courage as she could muster. She crawled into bed with him, tears streaming down her face. His face mirrored her own. Gently, she placed her hand on his heart, just as the voice had instructed her to do. Carolanne's arm tingled. She felt a humming vibration pour from her heart, course down her arm and through her hand. It felt like a jolt of electricity. His eyes met hers and he gasped. *Something shifted.* She couldn't explain what had happened, but the energy in the room shifted. The expression on his face shifted. Something inside of her shifted. The energy between them shifted.

"I don't know what you just did, but I feel like I just got my soul back," Joey said, his voice trembling and his eyes wet with tears.

Holy shit, what just happened? she wondered in shock and amazement. Without a moment's pause, Carolanne leapt out of the bed and bounded straight into her daughter's bathroom. She knocked the toilet seat down abruptly and plopped down to sit on it. *What the hell just happened?!* She couldn't believe it was real. The vision, the voice... all of it. Part of her had thought it was just her imagination, until now.

She took a couple deep breaths and gathered herself together. She went back into her daughter's bedroom and took a long look at her husband, studying him.

"You okay?" He asked tenderly. His eyes were soft. Color flushed his cheeks. The distant, empty look that had become a permanent part of his gaze was now gone. His energy had lifted. He seemed lighter, but at the same time more grounded.

She nodded. She was speechless.

"I love you so much. I don't want to go. Please don't make me go," he pleaded.

"I don't know what I want right now. We've had an emotional couple of days. Let's just take it one day at a time until we figure this out." She was still in shock. She wasn't sure how it would play out for them. But if his soul was really back in his body, she was willing to reconsider. Running programs... the ego... soul not in the body... her exchange with Joey's spirit in her vision... all came flooding back to her. It all made sense. But was it possible? It explained everything. But could it be true? She allowed herself to lean into the feeling of hope again. What she didn't know in that moment, but that she later came to realize, was that this was the start of his spiritual awakening.

That happened in the early hours of a quiet Sunday morning. Later that Sunday, the kids came back home from their sleepover party. They were dog tired. It was easy to act like nothing had happened in front of sleepy, exhausted kids. So they did. They didn't tell the kids about their impending separation. Was it even still impending? Carolanne didn't know. They decided to just take it one day at a time.

On Monday, the kids went to school as usual. Joey stayed home. He was still out of work. They talked some more, heart to heart. They also did some healing work on themselves and each other.

On Tuesday, Joey got a phone call saying that a company was creating a job they had never had before and wanted him to fill the position. He took the job, with his whole heart, and his body full of soul. The energy of their marriage continued to shift right before Carolanne's eyes.

For nearly a full year following their breakdown/breakthrough, Joey worked with Carolanne diligently to remove each program of self-destruction in his life using the HEAL Technique®, peeling back layer after layer. They did a lot of sessions together. A whole lot.

Now it has become a practice, something they work at every day. It has been so worthwhile. Today, Joey is transformed. He has found great success in all areas of his life– as a father and as a husband, in his career, personal health and finances. Joey is transformed and fully present for his life. He's living from his heart– his full heart.

If you're not living from the heart, you're really not living. If your body is not full of your soul, there's no point to being here. The fact is, you're not really here anyway.

CUTTING-EDGE INFO ABOUT YOUR HEART

The heart is a marvelous, miraculous organ. It pumps life-giving blood throughout our bodies, providing oxygenation and nutrition. The heart is the first organ to come into manifestation when we come into physical form. It's the first organ that develops in a human embryo. The heart forms and starts beating even before the brain begins to develop. But your heart is more than your body's most important organ. It's the seat of your soul, and the seat of your power. Did you know that your heart has a level of intelligence all its own that scientists are only just beginning to comprehend?

According to the Institute of HeartMath, the heart has 40,000 sensory neurons involved in transmitting information to the brain. In fact, your heart communicates more information to your brain than your brain communicates to your heart.[19] That's pretty influential. Using the innate wisdom of the heart, we can teach our brain new ways to think. We can bring our brains into alignment with our hearts. We only need to lead from the heart.

According to The Institute of HeartMath's research, your heart generates a powerful electromagnetic field just like your brain does, but the strength of the heart's electromagnetic field is unparalleled. It generates the largest electromagnetic field in the body, which is many, many times more powerful than that generated by the brain. The electromagnetic field of the heart as measured by an electrocardiogram (ECG) is sixty times greater than the amplitude of brainwaves measured in an electroencephalogram (EEG). The heart's magnetic field can be detected several feet away from the body, and changes according to your emotions.[20]

The Institute of HeartMath is doing some amazing research in this area. In their study *The Electricity of Touch: Detection and Measurement of Cardiac Energy Exchange Between People*, researchers found that the heart's potent electromagnetic field can be detected several feet away from a person's physical body. They have even measured the electromagnetic frequency of the heart's field when exchanging information between two people in close proximity.[21] That means others can pick up on the state of your emotions through the electromagnetic energy of your heart!

We are powerful, we are energy, and the most powerful energetic field generator in these radically awesome physical bodies of ours is our heart. Remember our donut-shaped toroidal energy fields? Our hearts produce the biggest, mightiest, most impressive donuts. On the level of the physical body, breath regulates the heart, and the heart generates the most powerful electromagnetic field around us. So it stands to reason that at the level of our physical bodies, breath is the key for changing our field. Yoga, martial arts, tai chi, qigong, breath work and the meditation traditions are all centered in this knowledge.

The Institute of HeartMath's research shows that the heart's electromagnetic field contains certain information or coding, which is transmitted throughout the body and beyond. One of the thrilling findings of this research is that intentionally generated positive emotions can change the coding. Not only can we change this bio-energetic field surrounding our physical body with breath work, we can impact it on an emotional level by consciously working with our emotions. The most effective way to do this is by coming back into the heart.

LOVE OR FEAR?

There are two basic driving forces for everything we do: love and fear. In any moment of your life and with every situation, you have to choose how to respond. You can respond either out of love, or out of fear. In this present moment, the only decision you ever really have to make is whether to act out of love or out of fear.

Living from the heart is about choosing love, over and over and over again. Living from the heart means living and loving with your full heart. It means leading with love. Love is not joy or happiness. It is not an emotion. It is not an action. Love is a state of being. Living from the heart means living in this state of love.

Living from the heart means being fully present in your body. Your spirit comes into the body from the heart. The heart is often called the seat of the soul because it is the connecting point between our physical body and our non-physical soul.

Living from the heart means letting go of the need to be in control, which comes from fear or ego. It means opening your heart and having the courage to be who you really are, warts and all. It means letting go of what other people think or expect from you. Living from the heart means practicing self-love and self-compassion. It means disconnecting from judgment, from the self or otherwise. Living from the heart means fully feeling your emotions. It requires stillness so that you can tune in to your inner voice, the voice of your heart. It means trusting and honoring the wisdom of your heart. Living from the heart requires the practice of gratitude.

Our minds are so thoroughly programmed. Spiritual data cannot get in beyond the filter of the mind with all of its conditioning. The HEAL Technique®–using the intelligence of the heart–helps to clear that programming so that you can transform and evolve. The only way to break free from our own reactive patterns is to reconnect with our own heart's innate intelligence.

Let's face it– sometimes the ego wreaks havoc in our lives. It doesn't mean to. Ego is what gives us our sense of self. We believe it gives us our identity, but this is really just a case of mistaken identity. It tells us we are separate. It misleads us. Not intentionally, but it still does. It wants us to believe that our limited little egos make up the whole of who we are, *and we often believe it.*

You see, the ego wants desperately to be in charge. It likes to tell you that it's the boss. It fights like hell to keep itself in power. Think of your ego as your inner temper-tantrum-throwing three-year-old. Like any overeager, over-stimulated child, the ego sometimes participates a little too enthusiastically when it would really serve you more if it would just go and take a nap. Just like anything out of balance, what your ego really needs is love.

The ego gets a bad rap. It's not a bad part of us. It really is like a child. It's vulnerable. It feels so separate. It's just running programs. Your little ego thinks it is doing a perfect job of granting a sense of individuality to your experiences. And it is. We just get out of balance when we believe that the ego is the whole of who we are. We get out of balance whenever we polarize to one side or the other.

Begin to observe yourself and your different parts. Notice that all these different parts of yourself have different voices, different agendas, different desires. Observe them all. Begin to distinguish the voice of your ego from the other aspects of you. Get in tune with the quiet voice of your heart. Listen closely to the wise voice of your higher self. Observe these precious parts of you. Then observe who is doing the observing– *All you.* All magnificent, beautiful, brilliant you.

The heart is the doorway to balancing the ego. Anything that is out of balance just lacks love. Think of your ego like a little child that you are in love with. Teach it like a child. Retrain the ego to come from a place of pure, unconditional love. If the ego is getting all tough-talking and bossy, just show it some love. Put it right in the middle of your heart. Imagine your little ego sitting there inside your mind, a hard little marble. Gently move that little marble from the center of your mind, down your throat, and plug it into the center of your soft and squishy heart. Feel your heart envelope that little ego-marble into a bear hug of an embrace, surrounding it with pure unconditional love. The magic is in the balance. Love is the ultimate balancer.

We are so cerebral and so conditioned to live from our heads that living from the heart takes conscious, deliberate, disciplined practice, at least at first. The ego tries to keep you trapped in the programs. It doesn't allow you to just be. It's the voice inside that says you are not enough. But it is an illusion. It's just a program. Ego chatter, brain analytics, worrying about the past, fretting over the future, judgment, fear… all of these are constructs of the mind. When you are experiencing these things, you are in your head. When you're in your head, you're on a rollercoaster of ups, downs and all-arounds. It pushes and pulls you in all directions. Your brain can be quite brilliant, confidently displaying logic and reason, capable of understanding complex calculations and theories. The problem is that it is not in touch with your deepest feelings, or the deepest parts of you. Our brains get power hungry and our lives get out of whack. For most of us, it's true that our lives are out of balance because we live from our heads. Although it sounds overly simple, getting into your heart is the key to balancing all aspects of your being.

Only love is real anyway, so the only real choice is love.

LIVING FROM THE HEART AS A PRACTICE

Living from the heart is a choice. Not a choice that you make once, but a choice that you have to make over and over again, every moment. Living from the heart is a practice, like yoga or playing the piano. The more you do it, the more natural it becomes. It has to be practiced every day. Every moment, even from moment to moment. If you find yourself thinking, *Oh my God, I'm not living from my heart*, there's no reason to freak out just yet. This doesn't mean you're not an authentic person, and it doesn't mean you are destined to live an inauthentic life. Rather, it means you are conscious now and get to choose how you will live from this point forward. You will have many more opportunities to make this choice. Every moment, in fact.

Living from the heart is a discipline, and it takes discipline. You have to train yourself to live from the heart, through practice. You have to train your ego to be an integrated part of you instead of being owned by your ego. Again, this takes practice. This can be achieved by becoming an observer of yourself, by taking notice when you are not in your heart and continually bringing yourself back home to your heart center. Take notice when your ego is ruling the roost and just simply plug it back into your heart for integration. This can be done by opening your heart, inviting in and integrating the ego, without judgment or shame.

WHAT IT LOOKS LIKE TO BE OUT OF YOUR HEART:

How do you know when you are not in your heart? When you are running programs of the ego. You know the ones:

Judgment, toward yourself or others, or anything, really.

Perfectionism: The need to be right. The need to win. The need to control what others think of you. The need to control anything and everything.

Scarcity: The need to have more. The belief that you don't have enough. The belief that you are not enough. The need to be more. Feelings of unworthiness.

Numbing: Escapism. Addiction to food, drugs, alcohol, sex, gambling, or whatever else you may use to numb or escape.

Martyrdom: Making a great show of suffering or sacrifice in order to get attention, sympathy or glory. Read between the lines: Stealing energy. Being an attention whore.

Feeling disconnected: Separate. Less than or more than.

Shame: Self-punishment. Pain. Heart closing.

Your story. Whatever your story is, this is your ego's way of seducing you with illusion and distortions, which keeps you out of your heart.

Defending people, values, or beliefs.

Being offended creates the same harmful energy that offended you in the first place. It's your ego that gets offended.

Self-importance: Feeling superior. Feeling inferior.

WHAT IT LOOKS LIKE TO BE IN YOUR HEART:

Your heart is at the core of your being, both literally and symbolically. The heart is the center of ourselves. Staying in your center–in your heart–is the foundation of living a balanced life and creating balance in your body.

How do you know when you are in your heart?

Authenticity: You are authentically yourself and have authentic personal connections.

Being present: Your soul is fully present in your body. You are fully present for your life.

Gratitude: You feel genuinely grateful, from the bottom of your heart.

Peace: You feel peace, even in the midst of chaos.

Belonging: You feel a sense of belonging just from being, not from doing anything in particular.

Curiosity: When curiosity replaces judgment. When you can say, "I'm curious as to why I am feeling this way..." instead of condemning or judging yourself for it. Curiosity softens the ego.

Compassion toward yourself and others. Kindness toward yourself and others.

Self-observation: When you are able to notice that you have slipped back into ego programs without shaming yourself for it.

Surrender: Allowing things to unfold organically. Letting go of the need to control.

Serendipity: Connecting with the divine. Understanding that there are no accidents or coincidences. Knowing that everything is meant to be.

Intimacy with yourself and others. Willingness to be honest, truthful and vulnerable.

Self-love: Expressing and honoring your boundaries and limits. Practicing compassion and kindness toward yourself.

Purposefulness: When you are connected with your heart, you are also connected with your soul's purpose. When you are connected with your soul's purpose, you are on a purposeful life path.

HOW TO COME BACK INTO YOUR HEART

It's inevitable. We are going to fall back into old programs and patterns from time to time. That's why living from the heart is a practice. We keep working at it until we have more moments of living from the heart than not. Understand that occasionally you are going to fall off the heart wagon. We all are. Have compassion for yourself when you do. Here are four simple steps to help you to come back into your heart:

1. Observe yourself.

Become a conscious observer of your thoughts, feelings, behaviors, habits and patterns. Just witness. Become conscious of how present you are. Could you be more present? Witness the programs you are running. Are you living in judgment and shame, or feeling imprisoned by the limitations of your story? Does perfectionism have a stronghold on you? What about scarcity consciousness? Are you feeling disconnected? Offended? Defensive? Are you numbing yourself to your emotions? Are you playing the martyr? Feeling inferior or superior? Notice where your consciousness lies. The key to shifting in the midst of running programs is being able to notice that you are in them, without judgment or shame because those are programs, too.

2. Focus on your heart.

Close your eyes. Put your hands on your heart. Sometimes it helps to tap your chest above your heart to focus your energy there. Visualize the ego as a little marble in the center of your head. Does it have a color? Imagine dropping that marble down your throat and placing it lovingly into the center of your heart.

The key is to get into your heart. The mind is deeply programmed and conditioned. Your heart is your true guide. Sometimes, just shifting the focus of your attention away from your mind and into your heart helps you tune in to what is truth for you. Put your hands on your heart and tune in to the *thump-thump, thump-thump* of this profound organ, pumping life-giving, rich, oxygenated blood to your body. Feel the pulse and rhythm of your heartbeat. This is your pulse of power. Be still. Quiet your mind. Stay with it. Come back to it any time you feel out of sync.

3. Breathe deeply.

Breath regulates the heart, bringing it into a steady rhythmic rate. This, in turn, regulates your most powerful energy field and the information you are beaming out into the universe, which is just going to boomerang right back to you at some point in time and space.

Breath is the vital link to awareness, energy and transformation. Consciously and mindfully focusing on your breath brings you back into the present moment. It focuses your attention and energy back into the physical body, allowing you to anchor your soul in your heart.

Taking a few deep breaths forces you to slow down so you don't react based on your programming. It allows you to consciously choose how you are going to respond.

Breathe slowly. Breathe deeply, from the belly. Exhale for longer than you inhale, if you can. Take three breaths, or thirteen, whatever you need to center yourself in your heart.

4. Choose consciously.

You've become a witness to your own programs. You have consciously focused your energy on your heart. You have slowed down with conscious breathing. Now choose. How do you want to respond in this moment? How does your ego want to respond? How does your heart want to respond? What will you choose?

This little exercise will help you to get into the practice of centering yourself back into your heart. Consistent practice will decrease the pull of your ego programs and patterns, which will make the journey of coming back into your heart easier each time you choose it. It's like a muscle—work it and it gets stronger.

How do you stay more permanently in a space of open-heartedness? By discovering why you closed it, then healing it. That's what the HEAL Technique® will help you do.

6) YOU ARE VIBRATING: *Measuring Your Vibrations*

Everything is energy. You are energy. You have an energy field flowing in, through, and all around you. This energy field is connected to all other energy fields. We are all connected.

This flow of energy informs your DNA, your life blueprint, and the universe at large. Everything that is, was or ever will be–the field of pure potential–is written into an energy record of the collective unconscious. You are connected to that field.

Believe it or not, you have access to all of the information encoded in this field of energy right at your fingertips. Your body is a vehicle that is able to access that field of information. It's also a vehicle that may access the mysteries of your own subconscious mind. Your body is the hardware. Through the hardware of your physical body, you can access all of the hidden software and programs of the collective unconscious, including your own subconscious mind.

Whenever you focus your attention on a situation, your body will always be ready for you and will be there to assist. Even if you've injured your body or your body is aging, you can rely on your body as a vehicle to access information. The only obstacle that stops you is another part of you– your mind. But your body always tells the truth. There are untold numbers of ways to use your body's hardware to access your mind. We'll cover a few simple ones here: muscle testing, tipping, and using your intuition.

MUSCLE TESTING

Our nervous system is an antenna, which is able to distinguish subtle frequencies that your conscious mind–and a lot of scientific instruments– just can't measure. Muscle testing is a simple way to leverage your body's hardware in order to gain access to your subconscious. Anyone can do muscle testing. It doesn't require special training or a degree. You can muscle test yourself, or you can muscle test a partner. If you have never muscle tested before, we suggest finding a partner and experimenting first.

Always start by stating your intention to talk only to the physical body, and asking permission if you can talk to the physical body. Why? Because the mind will give you mind shit. Your body has the imprint of every memory, experience and emotion you have ever had. When muscle testing, trust the innate intelligence of your physical hardware.

MUSCLE TESTING A PARTNER

There are several ways that you can muscle test a partner. Experiment with these two approaches and see what you like best:

1. **Arm Muscle Test:** Stand facing each other. Have your partner raise her arm either directly in front of her or to the side at shoulder height. Make sure her arm is straight. Place two fingers above the wrist of your partner's outstretched arm.

   - Tell her to resist and push down on her arm. This will give you an idea of her baseline strength.
   - **Always start by stating your intention to talk to the body and asking permission**: "I want to talk to the physical body. May I talk to only the physical body?"
   - **Test for Positive Response:** While instructing your partner to resist say, "Can I get a 'yes'?" Push down on her arm. The muscles should remain strong for a "yes" response– you shouldn't be able to push her arm down.
   - **Test for Negative Response:** While instructing your partner to resist say, "Can I get a 'no'?" Push down on her arm. You should be able to push down on it noticeably more, because the muscles should weaken for a negative response.
   - **Test for Positive Response:** While instructing her to resist, tell her to say, "My name is ____," having her say her real name. Push down on her arm. It should remain strong because this response is truth.

- **Test for Negative Response:** While instructing her to resist, tell her to say, "My name is _____," directing her to say your name or any name that is not her own. Push down on her arm. You should be able to push down on it noticeably more, because the muscles weaken for any response that is not truth.
- Experiment with this kind of muscle testing using other truths and lies.

2. **Finger Muscle Test:** Face each other either sitting down or standing. Make sure both of you are comfortable and no legs are crossed. Take your partner's non-dominant hand. Ask him to press the tip of his middle finger and thumb together, forming a circle. Using both hands, loop the fingers of one hand around his thumb and the fingers of your other hand around his middle finger.

- Tell him to resist while you try to pull his thumb and middle finger apart with your fingers. This gives you a feel for his baseline strength.
- **Always start by stating your intention to talk to the body and asking permission**: "I want to talk to the physical body. May I talk to only the physical body?"
- **Test for Positive Response:** While instructing your partner to resist say, "Can I get a 'yes'?" Attempt to pull apart his thumb-middle finger loop. The muscles should remain strong for a "yes" response– you shouldn't be able to pull the thumb and middle finger apart.
- **Test for Negative Response:** While instructing your partner to resist say, "Can I get a 'no'?" Attempt to pull apart his thumb-middle finger loop. You should be able to pull the thumb and middle finger apart easily.
- **Test for Positive Response:** While instructing him to resist, tell him to say, "My name is _____," having him say his real name. Attempt to pull apart his thumb-middle finger loop. The muscles should remain strong because this response is truth– you won't be able to pull the thumb and middle finger apart.
- **Test for Negative Response:** While instructing him to resist, tell him to say, "My name is _____," directing him say your name or any name this is not his own. Attempt to pull apart his thumb-middle finger loop. Because the muscles weaken for untruth, you should be able to pull the thumb and middle finger apart.

- Experiment with this kind of muscle testing using other truths and lies.

You can test for lots of different things: foods, supplements, emotions, memories or thoughts. Have fun. Play with it until you get a good feel for how muscle testing works. Here are some more ways you can experiment with muscle testing:

- **FOOD:** Muscle test foods to learn which ones are the best for your unique body. Just for fun, hold an apple to your chest and muscle test. Then hold a candy bar to your chest and muscle test. Your body knows what is best for it.
- **SUPPLEMENTS:** Muscle test supplements to discover which ones are in alignment with your unique body's needs. One at a time, hold your supplements to your chest and muscle test. You might be surprised by what you learn!
- **EMOTIONS:** Muscle testing emotions is very enlightening because you can quickly see how your emotional state impacts your physical body. Think about someone you love, see his or her face in your mind and feel the emotions of your affection. When you can really feel the emotions in your physical body, muscle test. You should test strong because positive emotions like love strengthen us. Next, think about someone who has wronged you or made you angry. Think about what they did and how they made you angry. Really feel those feelings of anger. Then muscle test. Negative emotions like anger drain our strength.
- **MEMORIES:** Reflect on a happy memory, really visualizing it in your mind. Muscle test. Positive, happy memories give us strength in our bodies. Reflect on a negative memory and muscle test, and you'll find the opposite is true.
- **THOUGHTS:** Just like emotions and memories, positive, uplifting thoughts give us strength whereas negative thoughts weaken us. Test for yourself to see that positive thoughts lift our vibration and negative thoughts weaken our systems.

MUSCLE TESTING YOURSELF
After investigating muscle testing with a partner, test it out solo. Press your

thumb and one finger–we like to use either the middle finger or the pointer finger–together on your non-dominant hand, forming a circle. With your other hand, make another circle with your thumb and one finger– the same finger you used on the other hand, interlocking with the first circle you made so that the fingers of both hands are interlinked like a chain.

- Attempt to pull the finger link of your dominant hand through the finger link of your non-dominant hand at its weakest point, where the thumb and finger meet. That's how it works when muscle testing on your own.
- **Always start by stating your intention to talk to the body and asking permission**: "I want to talk to the physical body. May I talk to only the physical body?"
- **Test for Positive Response:** Say "yes" and try to pull apart pull your finger links apart. The muscles should remain strong for a "yes" response– your fingers should remain linked.
- **Test for Negative Response:** Say "no" and attempt to pull the links apart again. You should be able to break the link because muscles will weaken with a negative response.
- **Test for Positive Response:** Say, "My name is ____," and say your real name. Attempt to pull your finger links apart. The muscles should remain strong because it is truth– your links should stay intact.
- **Test for Negative Response:** Say, "My name is ____," and say a name that is not your own. Attempt to pull your finger links apart. Because the muscles weaken for untruth, you should be able to pull the links apart.
- Experiment with this kind of muscle testing using other truths and lies.

TIPPING

Another way to muscle test either solo or with someone else is to use tipping, or a sway test. With bare feet, or wearing flat shoes or sneakers, stand with your feet about shoulder width apart.

- **Calibrate your "yes" and "no."** First, you will have to calibrate your "yes" and "no" answers. Begin in neutral with your feet flat on the floor. Take a few deep breaths and relax. Close your eyes and become still.

> First, say out loud, "Yes, yes, yes, yes, yes, yes, yes." Say the word "yes" repeatedly until you become aware of your body either being pulled forward or being pulled backward. Make a mental note of the direction you tipped for your positive response– your body's "yes."

> Go back to neutral again and take three deep breaths. Relax in the initial neutral stance with your feet shoulder width apart and your eyes closed.

> Next, say out loud, "No, no, no, no, no, no, no." Repeat the word "no" until your body naturally sways forward or backward. Your negative response should take the opposite direction of your positive response. In other words, if you swayed forward for "yes," you should sway backward for "no."

- **Always start by stating your intention to talk to the body and asking permission**: "I want to talk to the physical body. May I talk to only the physical body?"

- **Test for Positive Response:** Say, "My name is _____," and say your real name. Notice if you are pulled forward or backward. The direction in which you sway for a true statement should be consistent with your positive response calibration. For example, if you swayed forward for a "yes" answer, your body should also tip forward for truth.

- **Test for Negative Response:** Say, "My name is _____," and say a name that is not your own. Notice which direction you sway towards. The direction in which you are pulled in response to a statement that is not true should be consistent with your negative response calibration. If you leaned backwards for a "no," you should also lean backwards for an untruth.

- Experiment with this kind of muscle testing using other truths and lies.

TROUBLESHOOTING FOR MUSCLE TESTING OR TIPPING

If you're new to muscle testing, it may seem tricky at first. You can always move ahead to the next section and engage your imagination and intuition. At the very least, just pretend. Pretending is the quickest route to intuition because it helps you to get out of your own way. If you are having a few hiccups with muscle testing or tipping, here are a few troubleshooting points:

1. If you find that you are getting a weak muscle response to a positive statement and a strong response to a negative statement, your polarities may be reversed. This means energy in the central meridian may be flowing in the wrong direction. Here are a few ways to correct polarity:
    *   If you're hungry or thirsty, eat something or drink a glass of water.
    *   Remove any metal that you're wearing. Metal may not affect the result at all, but if you're having challenges, remove jewelry and piercings. Even an underwire bra could block the flow of energy. If you have surgical implants or fillings, try some of the other tips listed. Take a few drops of liquid chlorophyll in water. Chlorophyll is the green pigment in plants that harnesses the sun's energy in photosynthesis. The chlorophyll molecule is chemically similar to human blood. It's a blood strengthener and may help the flow of energy in the body.
    *   Close your eyes, take a few deep breaths and set the intention to correct your polarity.
    *   Zip up your energy by making a zipping motion with your hand in front of your body, as if you are zipping up a big, puffy jacket.
2. If your results are inconsistent, here are a few more tips for troubleshooting:
    *   Drink a tall glass of water, at least sixteen ounces. Our bodies are electrical systems and water is a conductor.
    *   Rotate your ankles in a circular motion both clockwise and counterclockwise. This ensures that your energy is flowing smoothly.
    *   Walk on the earth barefoot. This connects you to the Earth's energy and grounds you.
    *   If you're hungry or thirsty, eat something or drink a glass of water.
    *   Remove any metal that you're wearing. Are you wearing an underwire bra, piercings or jewelry?
    *   Take a few drops of liquid chlorophyll in water.
    *   State your intention out loud to muscle test correctly.
    *   If you're tired, stressed, unfocused or under the influence, try drinking water and doing some deep breathing for five

minutes. If that doesn't correct it, stop and try again later when you're rested.

- Ask for assistance or divine guidance.
- Get your mind out of the way. If you think you know the answer or are trying to force a particular result, it will impact the accuracy of muscle testing. Test without attachment to the outcome and set the intention to get the truth. If you are still finding it difficult to get out of your own way, do a blind test. Here's how:
  - **Muscle testing with a partner:** Instead of conducting the muscle test by verbalizing your answers out loud, say them silently in your head and muscle test your partner. This will prevent his or her mind from getting in the way.
  - **Muscle testing with a partner:** Instead of verbalizing the answers, write all of the potential answers on individual slips of paper, fold them and mix them up. Muscle test holding each slip of paper one at a time, making a "yes" pile and a "no" pile. Then go back and look at results. This keeps both of your minds out of the way.
  - **Muscle testing yourself or tipping:** Write all of the potential answers on individual slips of paper, fold them and mix them up. Muscle test yourself or tip holding each slip of paper one at a time, making a "yes" pile and a "no" pile. Then go back and look at your results.

USING YOUR INTUITION

Albert Einstein said the intuitive mind is a sacred gift. He described intuition as a "feeling for the order lying behind the appearance of something."[22]

In addition to using your body to access answers and information encoded in your energy field through muscle testing or tipping, you can also use your body through intuition. Intuition is the ability to access reality or information beyond what may be interpreted by the five senses, going beyond the physical plane. Your ego is fearful of this because it can only perceive the world through the five senses. It cannot control what it cannot perceive. Therefore, it gets a little spooked when it comes to intuition.

Intuition is the ability to perceive beyond the limits and boundaries of the ego. Intuition doesn't stream to you like a thought, it just appears. It just "pops" in. It may pop into your mind or your body in the form of a feeling, color, image, impression, sensation, smell, taste or sound. It may just be a primitive feeling in your gut: A knowing. A quiet voice within. An internal nudge. A fleeting insight that you write off as "just your imagination." Oftentimes, intuition may come as a feeling deep in the gut. Feel into your physical body for your answers. These are all markers of the body's sensation of intuition.

Imagination is the capacity to have an experience beyond the physical experience. You can use your imagination to access intuition. If you find yourself struggling to get in touch with your intuition, just pretend that you can access it. Pretend that you're intuitive. Pretend that you know. Pretending is all it takes. Pretending removes judgment and quiets the ego. Pretending gives you direct access to imagination.

Intuition is the ability to access reality or information beyond what may be interpreted by the five senses. Imagination is the ability to have an experience beyond the physical experience, so it is in fact the experience of intuition. Just like thoughts are the experience of the mind and feelings are the experience of emotion, imagination is the experience of intuition. That's why Einstein also said, "Imagination is everything. It is the preview of life's coming attractions."[23]

HOW TO ACCESS YOUR INTUITION

Quiet your mind. Get centered. Take a few deep, slow breaths and relax. Get present in your body. Focus on inhaling and exhaling.

Set the intention to tune in to your intuition.

Pose your question and pay attention to what comes up. Stay open to flashes of insight, a-ha moments, pictures that pop into your mind's eye, or sudden sensations or impressions that you receive. This is all intuitive guidance revealed from within. Pay attention to your body's signals. A "yes" or positive response might feel light, while a "no" or negative response feels heavy. Tune in to your gut, and notice if it feels good, or bad, or cautious. Practice this, and over time you will become more fluent in your intuition's subtle and delicate language.

YOU ARE VIBRATING

All of existence is made up of the same basic stuff: energy. Energy is always in action– being born, unfolding, shifting and transforming. Consider yourself, your thoughts and your emotions in the context of an energy system. This energy system that is you can be measured and calibrated. Every thought, emotion and inclination you have can be energetically calibrated, along with its impact on your body. Each has an energy that will either strengthen or weaken you.

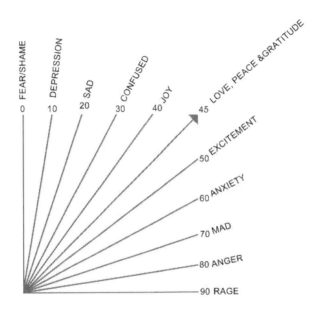

When we use the HEAL Technique®, we want to take an energetic "before" picture by calibrating your starting vibration in reference to whatever it is that you would like to shift. With starting vibrations, we're looking for two numbers– one on either side of the midline. That means you've got one number below forty-five and one number above it. When energy is stuck and you're out of balance, you split up the full spectrum of your vibration. This means your heart and mind are not in alignment. They're divided. So you'll find that your starting vibration has two numbers– one number between zero and forty-four and one number between forty-six and ninety. If your heart and mind were in alignment, you would be neutral, calibrate at a forty-five, and wouldn't need any work. Most of us aren't there in all layers of our life. Even if we are, stuff comes up that makes maintaining a state of unconditional love become a challenge.

Once the HEAL Technique® has been done, we calibrate an ending vibration to give you solid evidence that a shift has occurred. This is what you look like after your energetic makeover: beautiful and perfect and whole. The goal is to get to neutral– a forty-five. This is the frequency of love, peace and gratitude. It is true neutrality. From this vibration, you can see that everything is perfect. You love and accept exactly where you are on your path in this moment. You have gratitude for the pattern you are letting go because it helped you to learn and grow. You have gratitude for any suffering you may have endured because you are turning it into awareness and releasing the pattern.

Higher, faster vibrations always dissolve and convert lower, slower energies. When you get into the frequency of love, peace and gratitude, you have the power to transform everything in your life that you wish to shift.

7) YOU ARE FREQUENCIES: *Your Brainwave Frequencies*

When Carolanne first started experimenting with energy healing–and even when she experienced a miraculous healing herself–she was using a specific healing modality. When she applied what she had learned in her own self-healing in order to help others, she was surprised to discover that it worked for some people, but not for everyone.

She was disappointed, but not disheartened. She knew there was a reason, she just had to figure it out. An investigator by nature, she was determined to understand. She was unwavering in her belief that anyone could have an instant healing, and resolute in her quest to identify just how she could help everyone who needed it.

What makes one person experience a miracle and another stay stuck? What Carolanne uncovered is that it is all about codes. Each individual has a very specific vibrational code that is unique to them. You see, I can't use my code to heal you. You can't use your code to heal me. We have different codes. I can give you some of my energy to help fuel your battery, but then I'd be leaving myself with less energy. Not so good for me. Remember, we get sick or become miserable only if we lack energy.

That is why the world has energy vampires running around, sucking energy from everyone they come into contact with. You know the ones. It's easier to spot in someone else, but we all do it to some degree. We try to steal energy from others. Most of us don't do it consciously or maliciously. The truth is that most of it is subconsciously and unconsciously driven. It doesn't matter, the effect is still the same. Stealing energy is the source of all human drama, trauma and conflict in the world. It may look like gossip, guilt trips, judgment, criticism, competition, confrontation, controlling behavior, abuse, threats, sacrifice, boastfulness, intimidation, blame or manipulation. Even withholding emotion or energy is a form of stealing energy.

The person who gives their energy away will become depleted. With a lack of energy, they increase their likelihood of getting sick. If they get sick, maybe they will rest and recharge their battery. If not, perhaps they'll get even sicker. They will need to get energy from somewhere. They might steal energy from someone else and perpetuate the cycle. We all participate in this unconscious give and take all day long. A big energy exchange is always going on. Some of us are left with less than we started out with.

As we become more aware of how we exchange energy, we can become more and more responsible for our own energy. Instead of playing the stealing game, we can learn to generate our own energy by balancing ourselves and coming back into our hearts. The secret is in finding our own codes. The key to gaining insight into what your codes are lies in understanding the brainwave states.

THE FIVE BRAINWAVE STATES

We experience five different kinds of brainwaves that take us to different levels of consciousness– beta, alpha, theta, delta and gamma. Each of these brainwave states occurs at a specific frequency, which is measured in cycles per second (Hz). We all experience these brainwave frequencies at different times of the day or night, and at different times in our lives.

Beta (14-30 Hz)

The beta brainwave is the state of waking consciousness. You're alert, active and have the capacity for logic and reasoning. It's essential for normal, effective functioning in daily life. But spend too much time in this brainwave or get into the higher levels of beta and it translates into stress and anxiety. If you're talking to your boss, you're in beta. If you're playing tennis or giving a sales presentation, you're in beta. Beta is connected to your physical being.

Alpha (8-13.9 Hz)

The alpha brainwave frequency is slower than beta. Alpha is associated with relaxation. You might be having a nice little daydream, in light meditation, painting a lovely canvas or doing some visualization. It reduces stress, and enhances memory, concentration, creativity and learning. It's the doorway to your subconscious mind. The alpha brainwave state is connected to your emotional being.

Theta (4-7.9Hz)

Theta brainwaves are slower than alpha. The theta brainwave state is associated with deep relaxation, meditation and visualization, light sleep and REM dream states. This is the realm of your subconscious mind. This is where your deep-rooted programs reside. Theta is used in hypnosis. With direct access to the subconscious, this is where mind programming happens. In this powerful brainwave state, you are capable of massive inspiration, insight, and clarity. Theta is connected to your mental being.

Delta (0.1-3.9Hz)

Delta brainwaves are the slowest brain frequencies. Delta is associated with deep dreamless sleep, very deep meditation, restoration and healing. It's the realm of the unconscious. It's also the access point to the collective unconscious. When you receive information that's inaccessible consciously, it's being transmitted in the delta frequency– like when the phone rings and you know who is calling before you answer it. Delta is connected to your spiritual being.

Gamma (30-100Hz)

Gamma brainwaves are the fastest brainwave frequency. Gamma is associated with deep insight. You are able to see the big picture and all of the connections. It's connected to your God energy, the highest expression of your true self. Simply put, it's the frequency of your higher self. Gamma is also associated with increased levels of peace and happiness.

At the University of Wisconsin, neuroscientist Richard Davidson conducted experiments on Tibetan Buddhist monks and observed that they can enter the gamma brainwave frequency willingly in deep meditation. Not only that, monks may also enter into gamma when they are in a state of compassion and love.[24]

Athletes, musicians and performers are in gamma when they talk about being "in the zone." It's the state of consciousness that a basketball player is in when everything goes into slow motion and all he can see is the basket. The senses are all heightened, perception of reality is altered, and focus is intense. It also happens in traumatic moments, like car accidents, when it seems like time slows down and you can see the whole picture with striking clarity in slo-mo.

Gamma brain waves are fast. Crazy fast. In this state of consciousness, your brain is able to process ridiculous amounts of information at a super rapid rate. And that's not all. With gamma, you're also able to retrieve and remember information later. Search back through your own memory bank. The big moments in life and the big decisions all occurred in gamma. You know the ones I'm talking about. Memories from your moments in a gamma brainwave state spring into your mind easily, even right now as you are reading this, because they rise above the clutter like they are in HD Technicolor against a mostly gray backdrop. That's gamma.

Gamma waves influence the entire brain. Gamma brainwaves are able to make connections with information in all parts of the brain. Gamma frequencies speed back and forth, conducting a full sweep of the brain at an incredible pace. Gamma is powerful, and in this state of consciousness you have greater access to the many layers of your being.

THE BRAIN

The human brain is wildly complex. Since we're not neurosurgeons, I won't take a deep dive into the intricacies of the brain. We're really not capable of that kind of explanation anyway. Let's keep it simple. We have to at least take a peek because the brain contributes massively to your state of being. Most of us focus on our thought patterns or emotional state in order to become more healthy, happy and whole, but the truth is, our brainwaves play an integral part in the equation as well.

Imagine that the brain is a transfer box. It's constantly at work, sending electrical signals, communicating to other parts of the body, building new neural connections, processing data, and delivering messages in the form of hormones and neurotransmitters throughout the body. The electrical activity generated by the brain is, in fact, our brainwaves.

Every experience you have ever had, and every emotion you've ever felt, gets recorded and stored in your body courtesy of your brainwaves. When you experience an emotional charge, your brain tells your body where to store that charge on many different levels of your being. Your brain delivers these charges to the body. Your body will file this information according to your brain's unique brainwave frequency in that moment. Your brainwave frequency at the time of any super-charged emotional event influences the storage of that charge within you. That's the first key to your personal healing codes.

There are whole modalities based on this understanding. For example, in traditional Chinese medicine, it is believed that anger goes to the liver, resulting in the stagnation of liver qi. Anxiety may injure the lungs and large intestine, excessive mental stimulation is believed to cause imbalances in the spleen, grief may affect the lungs, and fear may impact the kidneys. Louise Hay has written a whole book on this called *Heal Your Body*, which is a wonderful healing resource that links different physical health challenges to probable causes in thought patterns and emotions.[25] Most healing traditions are built on the understanding that emotional stuff gets stored in the body and is the cause of disease and life's other challenges. We know it intuitively, too. That's why we say things like, "Grrr, the gall of that man!" or "That really pisses me off!" or "That really broke my heart." Hidden beliefs and emotions get stuck in the tissue. The brain is not the storage database, the whole body is.

THE FULL SPECTRUM OF YOU: SPIRITUAL, MENTAL, EMOTIONAL, PHYSICAL

Chances are, you're not just holding the charge in your physical body. You're likely holding it in another layer of your super-sparkly multi-dimensional self as well. If it shows up in the physical, most of the time it's also being held in the mental, spiritual or emotional body, too.

Your physical body is the most dense. Conventionally, we treat the physical with something physical. For example, if you're sick, perhaps you will try to heal with food, herbs or medicine. It's all physical. This means you are only treating it in a beta state. If the source is in fact only physical, then you'll respond to the treatment just fine. But what if the source of the imbalance is not in the physical? Chances are it will become very difficult to heal, or the healing may take a really long time.

Consider this: Before that ailment became physical, it was an emotional condition. Emotional conditions exist in the alpha brainwave state. You would have to have a lot of alpha frequency going on to have the condition condense and show up in the physical, with many emotions blocking the doorway of the subconscious, and metastasizing like a cancer.

Before this energy can manifest as an emotion, it has to first be a thought. This may not be a conscious thought. In fact, most of the time it's not conscious at all. Instead, it's our subconscious programming that influences our thought patterns, which in turn influences our emotional patterns. This is in the theta brainwave state. When you have so many emotions shoved so deeply into the unconscious, they sit there and metastasize, spreading to other areas of your body and being.

Before this energy becomes a thought, it exists in the spiritual. Your spirituality in your delta wave harnesses and holds all of your belief systems. Decisions that you've made in this life, past life experiences, ancestral karma and your genetic heritage all act as on/off switches. Beliefs and decisions from this life, past lives, and the lives of your ancestors determine what switches get flipped at any moment. Life is what triggers the switch. Your beliefs determine what gets flipped on and off: Wellness or disease. Prosperity or poverty. Feeling worthy or unworthy. Peace or chaos. Balance or instability. Happiness or depression. Love or fear. It all really just comes down to love or fear.

We think what ails us starts in our bodies (beta), our heads (theta), or in our emotions (alpha). But that's just because it's easier to be conscious of those things. We just don't know or understand the abundance of things that go on below the threshold of the conscious mind. We have a hard time grasping how much actually goes on in the spiritual– the delta or gamma frequencies. Almost all trauma, shock and extreme excitement puts us in a gamma brainwave state. Big life-altering moments and their corresponding charges almost always happen in gamma. That's why you can easily recall them when you think back through your life. It's the state in which time is irrelevant. These events get imprinted on us and change our belief systems in an instant in the subconscious. That's why they are life altering. The charges instantly embed and change the course of your life. They can't be cleared quickly and easily unless you are able to get back into the particular brainwave state in which they originally took place. That's why some healing modalities work for some people but not for everyone.

YOUR UNIQUE CODES
The HEAL Technique® uses a gamma brainwave frequency to access the

originating charge. Gamma is almost always the frequency you were in when you flipped a switch inside, when you turned something on or turned something off, when you started a new program or turned off an old one. Gamma is most likely the activation point. Gamma is the broadest spectrum frequency we can access, perfect for broad spectrum healing.

But what if the source of energy didn't originate in the gamma brainwave frequency? No worries. You're covered there, too. Remember that gamma brainwaves impact the whole brain, zipping back and forth at ridiculously fast rates, achieving full and complete sweeps of the entire brain. Gamma gives you access to all of it– all of the brainwave states and all aspects of your being.

Even if we only clear the energy in gamma, you're insured. But we don't just go to gamma to get the shift. We also find the specific brainwave frequencies that are influencing your situation and we go into those, too. We'll get to the unique root cause of what you want to shift this way.

The key to your unique codes is connected to the event that triggered your switches and jammed up your energy, your brainwave frequency when the event took place, the emotions you felt, decisions you made, and the energetic body or bodies affected. The HEAL Technique® guides you through a simple process to uncover the exclusive codes hidden within you, and guides you in the process of using your codes to open up the flow of energy, through your very own heart. I know the brainwave stuff can seem overwhelming, and the idea of finding the secret codes that you carry within your own being may seem unbelievable right now. It's just background info. The truth is, you don't need to understand any of it for the HEAL Technique® to work. In any case, we are building on knowledge here, and transmitting love through the frequency of the words you are reading. It's all leading up to someplace good and juicy, and hugely profound.

Once we've got your codes, you'll have the blueprint for clearing the pattern so you can clear it once and for all. No matter what, by the time you journey through the process, a shift will happen. Then everything can change. Limitations lift. You move into expanded awareness. You generate energy for yourself through your very own heart.

The process helps you to flip the switch. Turn off the switch on limitation and move into freedom. Turn off disease and flip on wellness. Move from scarcity to abundance. Sorrow to joy. Fear to love. Ultimately, it's just about bringing you back into balance in a state of love. That's zero point energy. That's neutrality. Remember, love is the ultimate balancing force.

NEUROPLASTICITY AND YOUR BRAIN

Whatever is not working in your life–your body, your relationships, your finances, your career, your spirituality, your whatever–is not working because your switch is flipped to a program that is not serving to fulfill your greatest desires for yourself in that area. You may consciously want it more than anything in the world, but under the surface you are running a program that is creating something else in your life to manifest completely. That program plays on a loop and becomes a pattern. The more that program does the loopity-loop, the stronger the neural pathways for that pattern in your brain will become.

Imagine going for a walk in the woods. You see a beaten pathway that others have walked. Perhaps some cars have even driven over it and have left tire tracks to follow. The grass is flattened and the bushes and trees have been cleared. It's the path of least resistance. It's easier to stroll on the path that's already there than to create a new path. Quicker, too. Your brain is kind of like that. Neuroscientists have a saying for this: "Neurons that fire together wire together." It's called Hebb's Law because Donald Hebb, a neuropsychologist, coined a similar phrase in 1949 that explained this phenomena: "Cells that fire together wire together."[26] That's neuroplasticity.

Our brain cells communicate with each other through a process called neuronal firing. This is when one brain cell releases a neurotransmitter that another brain cell takes in. When brain cells communicate frequently, their connection gets stronger and more reinforced, laying down a pathway. The more these messages travel the same path in the brain, the faster and easier it becomes to travel that path. It becomes the beaten path in the brain– the path of least resistance. Each belief we hold, each experience we have, all of our thoughts, feelings, and even muscle actions become embedded in the network of brain cells that initially generated that experience. Every time you think a thought, feel a feeling or take an action, you strengthen the connections for that particular thought, feeling or action in your brain's neural network. You encounter it in your life experience, which reinforces the neural net in your brain, strengthening the connections even further. It's a program running on a continuous loop in your brain's neural network, as well as a repeating pattern of experience in your life, creating a self-perpetuating cycle.

But that's just the dark side of neuroplasticity. Like everything in our reality, it also has a high expression. Neurons that fire together wire together. The brain has plasticity. You wired it in the first place, you just did it unconsciously. With your codes, you can consciously program yourself on all levels to create a new pattern and break the old one in the process. You can literally rewire your brain, no electrician needed, because neurons that no longer fire together will no longer wire together. When you quit hiking the same trail in your neural net, those connections weaken and die off. The grass starts growing and the brush gets thick. Over time, it's hard to see that a trail was ever there. You can consciously create new pathways. That's plasticity working for you, baby!

A critical first step to beginning the project of DIY brain rewiring is to raise your own level of consciousness so that you can be keenly aware of your thoughts, feelings and actions. The biggest challenge to laying down a new pathway in your brain is that much of what built the existing networks happened unconsciously, or was driven by the subconscious.

That's where the HEAL Technique® comes in. It brings the unconscious and subconscious elements of your programming up into the conscious mind. Once you're conscious of it, you can become an active participant in the development of your mind and brain. You can use the information that bubbles up from the subconscious to change the way you react, create, and respond. You can gain direct control of your own brain structure and reprogram it. You'll create new pathways in the brain and new experiences in your life. This is the ultimate expression of personal responsibility and empowerment.

See? I told you that you were freaking powerful!

8) YOU ARE EMOTIONAL: *Your Energy in Motion*

Emotions are energy in motion. Feelings are the experience of emotion– they're what you experience when you sense energy in motion. Emotions want to move through your body. Flow is the natural state. Unfortunately, we interfere with the natural flow of emotions moving through us. We fear our emotions, or we deny, repress, or judge them. This blocks the natural flow of emotional energy within us. Emotion then gets stuck in our bodies, creating energetic blocks.

In order to remove the blocks and clear a path for energy to flow again, it's absolutely essential to get downright real with our genuine emotions, even the yucky ones. *Especially the yucky ones.* Your emotions are the keys that unlock the code to your transformation. Clearing any kind of stuck energy requires you to uncover the buried layers of emotions, and expose them to the light of your consciousness. It's non-negotiable. This is true emotional excavation. Each layer takes you deeper and deeper into the subconscious patterns and belief systems that keep you stuck.

Don't get stuck in the mental chatter. Be careful to stay out of the story. You know that story that you tell yourself about your situation? Yeah, that helps to keep you stuck. The story is just your thoughts about it– it's all mental. Most people spend so much time talking about how they feel, to friends, family, therapists and anyone who will listen, but they don't actually *feel* their feelings. Analyzing and intellectualizing your feelings is not the same as feeling them. Talking about them is not feeling them.

Most people are afraid to really experience fully feeling their emotions. Maybe you're afraid of losing control. Maybe you're afraid of being vulnerable, or you're scared of feeling the pain of your feelings, or the feeling of loss or any other uncomfortable feelings that come with that emotion. Maybe you're even afraid to cry.

Your head is going to try to protect you from the pattern so it's important to *feel* your way through this and really get in touch with the feelings. Avoid going into the story that you tell yourself. That's just talking from your head and it won't help. In fact, it hinders you. Pretend you can take your brain and set it aside for just a bit. Just stick with the emotions. The source that feeds the energy to keep you stuck in this pattern is your emotions. *Stay with the emotion.* It must come through the gut and the heart. In your body, it may feel like it comes from the belly or solar plexus. Emotions never come from the head. If you have to think about your emotions, you're in your head. Emotions are felt, not thought of.

Let's try it right now. Think of something that makes you angry. Just notice what this thought is and where in your body you experience thinking about anger. Now *feel* the anger in your body. Notice the difference.

The best way to feel into your emotions is to close your eyes and put your hands on your heart. Or put one hand on your heart and one hand on your solar plexus. Do whichever feels good to you and whichever helps you to turn your awareness inward to your feelings.

Imagine or pretend there is a marble in the center of your brain. Imagine plugging that marble into your head. That's your ego, and we are just going to integrate it into the heart so it stays out of your way for the time being, by visualizing the ego as a little marble in the center of your head. Pretend it has a color and see that color in your mind's eye. Imagine dropping that marble down your throat and placing it lovingly into the center of your heart.

Now feel into whatever it is that you would like to shift. How does struggling with this issue make you feel? For example, if you want to find a mate, how does it make you feel that you don't have that person in your life? If you want to heal a physical ailment, how does having it make you feel? If your desire is to change careers, how does your current career path make you feel? If you want to create abundance, how does not having it make you feel? Get the idea?

Pay attention to what comes up. Is it a thought or is it a feeling? If it's a head answer, feel into it and find the feeling. You must find the emotion; emotions are the key that unlocks your personal codes. If you want to crack the code, you've got to feel the feelings.

Once you uncover that first layer of emotion, it's important to keep digging. Feel into the emotion. Sit in that emotion. Really stew in it and feel it. Then find the next emotion underneath that feeds the first one.

Your emotions are tiered like Legos, each block layered one on top of the other. This layering of emotions creates the pattern. The one on top is fed by the one underneath, which is fed by the one underneath that, and so on.

Excavate layer after layer of emotions, diving deeper and deeper into the subconscious until you find the source that feeds the energy of this pattern. The best way to peel back each layer of emotions is by feeling into the emotion and asking what's underneath. What's feeding the emotion? Imagine that you can pick it up and see what's under it. Feel into the emotion and ask yourself how that emotion makes you feel. Pretend you can peel back emotions like the layers of an onion and find what's underneath. Imagine being able to look inside the feeling, and find what feeds it.

Continue on in this pattern of peeling back one layer of heavy emotions after the next until you get to the root. You know you're at the root when you make a full circle back to the first emotion, or when you feel that you have uncovered them all. The bottom layer of emotion is the one that feeds all of the other emotions in your pattern. It's the root. It has the juice. Once you expose the root emotion to the light of your conscious awareness, it can't hide out in the crevices of the subconscious anymore. It loses some of its power.

The layered stack of your emotions reflects the exact same pattern that is in your DNA. It's also the same circuitry that runs in the neural network of your brain. It's the precise pattern that creates your energetic blockage. It's the exact frequency that holds the pattern in place. If you look closely, you'll see that this pattern wreaks havoc in many areas of your life.

It's not all heavy and bad, though. Often, we learn some pretty righteous things about ourselves by examining and exploring tough situations and heavy feelings. Rock bottom can be a springboard to new heights. Trials and tribulations teach you strength and resiliency. Compression often leads to expansion. You will need to take a look at the light, positive feelings that came as a result of the pattern, too, and examine how those good feelings buddied up with the heavy ones to help hold the pattern in place.

Something triggered the pattern: An event in your past. A decision you made. Some memory that holds a charge. You'll use the emotions and feelings of this pattern and follow them back to find the memory of a time and event when you first experienced the same feelings. That memory is what ignited the pattern– it flipped the switch in your DNA. The only way to eliminate the pattern is to uncover the codes. The only way to get the code is to feel through the pattern of emotions. No head stuff, all heart.

If you're struggling to find the words to represent your emotions, here's a list to help you out. Don't use your head. Feel into them with your heart.

HEAVY FEELINGS

SAD	FEAR	ANGRY	ANXIOUS
depressed	scared	enraged	restless
grief	terrified	irritated	nervous
sorrow	panicked	frustrated	worried
anguish	frightened	annoyed	stressed
despair	shaky	upset	frantic
desperate	afraid	hateful	concerned
unhappy	dread	bitter	uneasy
lonely	alarmed	resentful	panicked
discouraged		infuriated	tense
guilty		rage	edgy
dissatisfied		fuming	jumpy
miserable		agitated	frazzled
defeated		furious	pressured
despondent		livid	
discouraged	STUCK	mad	
down	suffocated	seething	
heavy	pressured	outraged	
remorseful	trapped	exasperated	
unfulfilled	stagnant		
unworthy	limited		
withdrawn	burdened		
melancholy			

HURT	CONFUSED	EXHAUSTED	ASHAMED
crushed	shocked	overwhelmed	embarrassed
betrayed	lost	intimidated	humiliated

pained	disillusioned	limited	shame
tortured	crazy	weak	unworthy
injured	insane	alone	
rejected	fragmented	paralyzed	
offended	paranoid	inferior	
wounded	perplexed	worthless	
devastated	doubtful	weary	
victimized	distrustful	empty	
heartbroken	skeptical	lifeless	
alienated	uncertain	apathetic	
tormented	conflicted	defeated	
abused		deprived	
agony		doomed	
anguish		heavy	
burdened		hopeless	
		powerless	

LIGHT FEELINGS

HAPPY	STRONG	PEACEFUL	LOVE
joy	brave	calm	open
grateful	courageous	comfortable	compassionate
overjoyed	determined	open	receptive
ecstatic	motivated	content	passionate
excited	bold	relaxed	touched
satisfied	daring	serene	sympathetic
elated	confident	blessed	empathic
optimistic	hopeful	blissful	loving
thrilled	empowered	centered	loved
spirited	powerful	clear	inspired
enthusiastic	worthy	harmonious	authentic
euphoric		balanced	aware
exhilarated		humble	connected
fulfilled		present	nurtured
hopeful			nourished
			light
			expansive

FREE	AWAKE	INTERESTED
liberated	abundant	intrigued
playful	enlightened	curious
energized	conscious	fascinated
impulsive	connected	inquisitive
emancipated	energized	engrossed
limitless	illuminated	creative
	renewed	eager

9) YOU ARE CROSS-WIRED: *Disentangle From the Program*

It happened again. Everything had been going smoothly at work, or so it seemed. Performance had been humming along. Drama was down to a minimum. There was an eerie sort of contentment in the air, which soon turned into complacency and stagnant energy. Everyone got a little too comfortable, which quickly started showing up as sloppy work and diminished performance. He should have known. This was a recurring pattern now. Every time he relaxed a little and it seemed like things were going well, George encountered drama of one sort or another. It really pissed him off.

It didn't seem like much to worry about at first, but soon the client complaints started pouring in. They weren't happy with the quality of the work. They weren't happy with the quantity, either. In fact, they complained about every little thing that they could find to complain about, and they were looking hard. A simple oversight here, an inaccuracy there. George was even blamed for things that were not his company's fault. He knew he was under a magnifying glass. He would have to shake things up and make some changes.

He called his entire staff into the conference room and let them have it. He ranted and raved. He threatened, pressured and intimidated. He wanted to light a fire under their asses. He wanted to motivate them to do better and be better. Fear was the tool that he used for motivation.

It worked, but only temporarily. Performance went through the roof that afternoon. It even continued throughout the rest of that week. But by the time the following Monday rolled around, energy had dwindled.

George got to work, digging into the operations of the business. He shifted his strategy. He modified his tactics. He restructured, fired and hired. He was angry as hell but he was making progress with the business. Clients were raving about their work. Their quality, productivity and results all improved significantly. Soon George's chest started hurting. He suffered from heart palpitations and insomnia. The stress just got to be too much. He recognized his own pattern. He had been here too many times before and was tired of it. So he went to Carolanne for a session.

"What would you like to shift today?" Carolanne asked him.

"Drama in my business and all of the anxiety, stress and insomnia that comes with it. I also feel really bad about reaming out my staff. I'm not proud of my behavior, but I was really angry." George told her the whole story and Carolanne listened patiently, occasionally jotting down a note or two. She was familiar with his business. She occasionally came in to work with his staff, to help shift the energy and help them to reach their career goals.

Carolanne began with muscle testing. "Give me your hand. Press the tips of your middle finger and thumb together. I'm going to try to pull them apart with my fingers and I want you to resist me. Your body will hold strong for truth. Your muscles will weaken for anything that is not true for you. Ready?"

George nodded and pressed the thumb and middle finger of his left hand together, forming a circle with his fingers. Carolanne grabbed his thumb with her right hand and his middle finger with her left. She calibrated for accuracy first.

"Say, 'I'm a man,'" she instructed him. He repeated the words and she pulled on his thumb and middle finger. They stayed strong and connected. Truth.

"Now say, 'I'm a woman,'" she requested. He felt silly, but said it anyway as she pulled again on his fingers. He weakened and she easily pulled them apart. Not truth. Good. She had established a baseline and he was muscle testing accurately.

Next she calibrated his starting vibration– the "before" picture. She consulted the vibration chart on her HEAL Technique® worksheet. (See p. 150) Pulling apart his fingers as she called out each number, she recited, "In reference to this situation with George's business, George is currently vibrating at zero." His fingers held strong and remained connected.

"Ninety," Carolanne said, pulling on his fingers again. Again, they wouldn't budge. Truth again. Zero and ninety correspond to fear and rage. No surprise there.

"In reference to this issue with his business, George's body full of soul is at one hundred percent," Carolanne said out loud and muscle tested. She easily pulled his fingers apart. Parts of his soul were not in his body. He was running programs to some degree. She continued to muscle test to find out exactly to what degree, working backwards from one hundred percent in increments of ten until he tested strong for truth. His body full of soul was at fifty percent. She jotted the number down on her HEAL Technique® worksheet.

"In reference to this business situation, George's self-love is at one hundred percent," she said out loud, pulling George's fingers apart simultaneously. He was not operating out of self-love. But how much was he missing?

"Self-love is at ninety percent," she checked, his fingers effortlessly pulling apart. Carolanne progressed through the numbers in decreasing order.

"Self-love is at eighty percent." Still weak.

"Seventy percent." Weak again.

"Sixty percent." Finally, his fingers held strong. She wrote the number in the corresponding space on the HEAL Technique® worksheet.

"George is ready for his organic life path at one hundred percent," Carolanne stated, muscle testing. He held strong. He was ready.

Next she tested for source. She needed to know if the blockage of energy was his, someone else's, or something else.

"Say, 'This is mine,'" she instructed. He repeated the words and Carolanne muscle tested him. Very strong. It was definitely his. She continued to test to see if it was also perhaps someone else's or something else. For both, his muscle test revealed weakness. It was his alone.

Next she tested to find the brainwave state the energetic blockage was in. This would provide guidance on the most beneficial type of breath work to use at the end of the session in order to clear it.

"This is in a beta," she tested, pulling his fingers apart. Weak. He couldn't hold them together. It wasn't in the physical.

"This is in an alpha," she repeated the muscle test, but this time he held strong. It was in the emotional.

"This is in a theta," she tested again. Strong again. It was also in the mental.

"This is in a delta," she tested. Weak. It wasn't spiritual. So it was in the alpha and theta brainwave states. She made a note of it that she would refer to again later.

"Close your eyes and put your hands on your heart. Feel into this situation in your business. When clients complain and your staff slacks, when there's drama at work, what feelings does that stir up in you? Also feel into your outburst with your team. How does that make you feel?" Carolanne mined the data of George's emotions.

"Angry," George responded harshly and without pause. He sure sounded angry.

"What is the intensity of that anger on a scale of zero to ten?" She asked.

"Eight," he answered.

"When you feel into that anger, how does that make you feel?" Carolanne continued.

"I feel so much pressure to make it all happen all of the time. It's too much," he answered.

"What's the intensity, zero to ten?"

"Ten."

"Good. What's underneath the feeling of pressure?" Carolanne persisted in uncovering layer after layer of emotion, energy and the intensity of the charges.

"Fear."

"Rate the intensity. Zero to ten?"

"Nine."

"When you feel into the fear, how does that make you feel?"

"Ashamed. I let the fear and pressure get the better of me. I really took it out on my team."

"How would you rate the intensity of that shame?"

"Six or seven at least."

"How does that shame make you feel?"

"Guilty. But I did it with the best of intentions. I thought it would help them do better," George explained.

"Zero to ten?"

"Seven."

"What's under the guilt?"

"Exhaustion and defeat. I am so tired of this. I want to give up."

"Intensity?"

"Eight."

"When you feel exhausted and defeated, how does that make you feel?"

"Angry and frustrated." George's voice was flat. He'd come full circle back to anger. Exhaustion and defeat were at the root of the emotional pattern.

"Good work, George," Carolanne encouraged. "Go ahead and keep your hands on your heart with your eyes closed. I want you to feel into the defeat and exhaustion. Where in your body are you storing these feelings?"

"In my chest. It's a tightness in my chest," George answered.

"OK, good. Now really feel into all that emotion again. I want you to tell me the first time you felt that sort of defeat and exhaustion. I'm going to count backwards from five to one and I want you to tell me the first memory that pops up for you. Five... four... three... two... one. Drop into that memory. When did you first feel these emotions?"

"When my first business fell apart. I made some really bad decisions. I created enemies. I felt like I hit rock bottom. I filed for bankruptcy. I lost my house. I almost lost my wife and kids," George revealed.

"What is the intensity of that memory, zero to ten?" Carolanne asked.

"At least an eight," he answered.

"OK, and through the whole process, what good things did you learn about yourself?" She dug deeper.

"About what I am going through now or when my first business went belly up?" he questioned. He wasn't sure what she was looking for.

"Either. Or both. The energetic pattern is the same. What did you learn about yourself when you felt angry, pressured, fear, shame, guilt, exhaustion and defeat in either situation."

"Well, I learned that I am motivated and driven. I didn't let the setback get me down," George reflected.

"Uh-huh. And how does it make you feel to realize that you are motivated and driven?" She was digging again.

"Excited. It makes me want to make stuff happen."

"And when you feel excited, what do you feel?"

"I guess I feel sort of renewed in my energy."

"Yes! And how does it make you feel to have renewed energy?"

"It makes me feel strong."

"What does feeling strong feel like for you?"

"It feels like joy."

"What do you feel when you experience joy?"

"I feel alive and awake."

"What does alive and awake feel like?"

"Motivated."

"Wow. Good work, George. You can open your eyes now. You just gave me all of your cheat codes. Listen to this. You've been running a pattern of energy that goes like this: anger, pressure, fear, shame, guilt, exhaustion and defeat. What you also told me was that your secondary gain from this pattern of energy is motivation and drive, excitement, having a renewed sense of energy, strength, joy, and feeling alive and awake. Now, watch this. Let me muscle test you. Ready?"

"Yup," he said and pressed his thumb and middle finger together again, thrusting his hand towards Carolanne. Again, she tested for accuracy.

"Say, 'My name is George,'" she instructed him. He repeated after her as she attempted to pull his fingers apart. They held strong for truth. Now she wanted to make sure they would weaken for an untruth.

"Now say, 'I'm riding a pink pony,'" she grinned. She loved messing with him.

"One of these days I'm going to come in riding a pink pony," George teased. He repeated the phrase and she pulled on his fingers again. He went weak. She separated his fingers without any effort. Perfect. He was still muscle testing accurately.

"Say, 'Anger gives me motivation and drive,'" she directed him again. He repeated after her, she pulled on his fingers and they remained strong. Truth. Very interesting.

"Now say, 'In order to feel excited, I must first feel pressure.'" He did and his muscles held strong again. Truth.

"Try this one on: 'In order to feel renewed energy, I must first feel fear.'" He repeated the words and realized they were true. His muscle test validated that.

"How about this: 'Feeling shame leads to feeling strong.'" George said it. Carolanne tested it. It was true, too.

"Say, 'Feelings of guilt lead to feelings of joy.'" Truth again.

"Say, 'I need to feel exhausted before I can feel alive and awake.'" He repeated the words, a little skeptically. How could feeling exhaustion lead to feeling alive and awake? Still, his muscles held strong, telling both

George and Carolanne that there were definitely some diametrically opposed cross-references embedded in his brain's neural network.

George couldn't believe it! This was the mess going on in his subconscious. No wonder he was having trouble in his business.

"So, George, what you've basically told me is that you have a pattern of creating certain heavy emotions in order to generate the energy for you to get to experience another set of unrelated emotions, but they're related for you. You need anger to get motivated, so you attract or create situations and experiences that make you angry, which gives you the energy for motivation. For you, feeling pressure stimulates you and is exciting. So you manifest situations in your life that put pressure on yourself, which creates energy and excitement," Carolanne explained.

"I had no idea," George marveled.

"I know. Aren't we humans funny?" she asked with a grin. Then she continued, "Let me finish telling you how funny you are. In order to get renewed energy, you need to feel fear, so your mind creates it. Bam! Instant renewal! Fear is your energy drink!"

"Wow." George was in awe, revelations popping off like crazy in his mind. The picture was becoming more and more clear.

"In order to feel strength, you must first feel shame. You actually create self-shaming experiences so you can feel strong."

"Don't want to do that anymore!" George declared.

"Don't worry, we're going to clear it. You want to hear more?"

George nodded and Carolanne continued, "Before you can feel joy, you must first feel guilt. In order to feel awake and alive, you have to first feel exhausted and defeated. Your brain has somehow cross-wired all of these emotions together."

"That makes sense," he agreed. "When my first business failed, I was devastated. But I took all of that anger and fear and leveraged it as the fuel to start over fresh and build something new. I thought it worked. I thought I was using all that bad stuff for a good cause."

"It did work, temporarily. But it's a short term fix, like caffeine and sugar. Eventually you're going to crash," she explained.

"I'm crashing now…" George realized.

"Well, how would you like to untangle the energy between these connections so that you can experience motivation, drive, excitement, renewed energy, strength, joy, and feeling alive and awake without having to go through the heavy emotions to get there? Imagine if you could reclaim all of the energy you have given away to feeling all of those negative emotions. Would you like to do that?"

"Absolutely," George answered instantly.

"OK, close your eyes," Carolanne instructed. "Put both hands on your heart. Tune in to the energy of your heart. We're setting the intention to clear this pattern at one hundred percent on all layers, all levels, and in all combinations. We're also setting the intention to neutralize the memories that ignited this pattern. We're setting the intention that George will reclaim all of the energy that has been leaked by this pattern."

She took a long breath in and continued, "Now, imagine that there is a hard little ball or marble inside of your head, right in the middle of your brain, right in between your eyes. Do you see it?"

"Uh-huh," he murmured, nodding.

"Good. What color is it?" She asked.

"Blue," he answered after a pause.

"OK, now what I want you to do is take that little blue marble and let it take a little elevator ride right down your throat and into the center of your heart. Imagine plugging it right into the middle of your heart and notice your heart radiating beams of light like the sun. See it?"

George nodded again.

At the start of the session, George's body revealed that the pattern was stuck in the alpha and theta brainwave states, which correspond to the emotional and mental bodies. This knowledge would guide the breath work. First they would start with nose-nose breaths to clear theta and the mental. Then they would progress to mouth-nose breaths to clear alpha and the emotional.

"OK, time to breathe and clear it. We're going to start with thirteen breaths in through the nose and out through the nose. Make the first twelve super deep, filling up and emptying the lungs completely. Hold the thirteenth breath as long as you can– that one takes you to gamma. It's the doorway to a new consciousness. Ready?" she asked, scooting her chair back to make space.

George nodded and did the same.

"Go ahead and take your fingertips and begin tapping on your sternum," Carolanne instructed. George began tapping.

Together they did twelve nose-nose breaths, cleansing and clearing the patterns tucked away in the theta brainwave frequency and the mental body. A completed cycle.

"Last one," Carolanne told him as she breathed in through her nose. "Hold it," she reminded him.

He drew in the last breath, holding it, then swallowed it down into his belly. Oxygen penetrated his whole being. When he couldn't hold his breath any longer, he let out an extended, exaggerated exhale through his nose. He felt light-headed and dizzy. His eyes remained closed until he felt steady again. Then they fluttered open and he looked right into Carolanne's bright blue eyes. She was grinning from ear to ear.

"Goooooood," she cooed. "We have one last breath exercise. This time, thirteen breaths in through the mouth and out of the nose. Same thing. Take big, huge, deep breaths in, sucking in oxygen through your teeth so I can hear it. Exaggerate it. When you blow it out, exhale hard through the nose. Hold the thirteenth breath and get ready for a whole new level of being! Here we go... breathe in... breathe out..."

Carolanne and George did the mouth-nose breaths together, clearing the pattern in the theta brainwave state and the corresponding mental body. George held the thirteenth breath, swallowing it down. He marinated in that last breath, delivering healing oxygen all over as it mopped up the stuck energy. When he could no longer hold it, he blew it out of his nose. He imagined that he was blowing the pattern away.

George remained still with his eyes closed as he felt the life-giving oxygen flowing through his body. He felt dazed, almost high. It felt so surreal.

"Let the dizzies work for you," Carolanne advised.

A few minutes later, when the wooziness subsided and George finally felt grounded again, he opened his eyes. Something had definitely shifted. He felt centered and calm. All of the anger and fear had left him. Then he yawned. Carolanne smiled.

She quickly recalibrated vibrations to show George how he had shifted.

"When we began, your starting vibration was a zero and ninety, fear and rage. Let's see where you are now," she said, reaching for his hand to muscle test.

"In reference to George's situation with his business, he is vibrating at a forty-five," she tried to pull his fingers apart. They held strong. He was in a vibration of peace, love and gratitude. Just to prove her point, she yanked on his fingers again. Super strong.

"George's body full of soul is now at one hundred percent," she stated, pulling on his fingers again. They wouldn't budge. He was back in his body, completely and fully present now, no longer running a program.

"George's self-love is at one hundred percent," she continued. Again, he held strong.

"Go ahead and close your eyes again. Put your hands on your heart. George, when you feel into this situation going on with your business, what is the intensity of that anger now?" Carolanne asked him.

"Nothing. It's not intense anymore," George answered.

"Feel into the pressure. What's the intensity?" Carolanne continued.

"Zero," he said.

"Feel into the fear you had. What's the intensity of that emotion?"

"Zero."

"What about your feelings of shame?"

"It's gone. Zero."

"Feel into your guilt. What's the intensity?"

"None," he replied.

"What about exhaustion?"

"Gone," he answered, and then opened his eyes. "Amazing. It all feels so completely neutral that I can't believe I was worked up about it at all."

A LITTLE BIT MORE ON NEUROPLASTICITY

We know that neurons that fire together will wire together. In addition to creating a well-trodden path in the neural network of your brain, neuroplasticity also tells us that our brains create associations by coincidence. It strengthens neural connections between beliefs, thoughts, feelings and actions even if they are not necessarily directly related at first. Your brain just links them together through association because they occurred at the same time as each other. Essentially, your brain assumes them to be connected and buddies them up in the network.

Every time you think a thought, feel a feeling or take an action, a group of neurons fire off in your brain. That creates a pattern– a buddy group that always wants to play together because they remember playing together once or twice before and decided it was fun. It basically strengthens the relationship between that particular set of neurons. The likelihood of that pattern firing together again increases each time they play together, because they pay closer attention to their associated buddies and build stronger ties to them. Over time, the buddying up of these associated neurons creates a really strong bond. The slightest activity on one neuron will trigger all the other neurons associated with it to fire, too. They become besties. They go everywhere together. You never see one without the other. They finish each other's sentences.

This is so common. It happens all the time below the level of the conscious mind.

Have you ever felt guilty for dreaming really, really big? Or for wanting something different for yourself? Like wishing for something different feels as if you're not appreciative of everything you have?

Guess what? You're crossing wires.

Have you ever gotten angry in order to get motivated to take action? Have you ever caught a little virus–or pretended to–to catch a little down time? Or gotten sick–or pretended to be–to get attention?

Wires crossed again.

We see it everywhere. I was once in a parenting class with a behavior analyst who was talking about parents' behaviors when cross-wiring showed up. She explained that parents often use psychosomatic illness, or even real pain and illness, to avoid dealing with difficult behaviors in their children. In her practice, she regularly sees mothers of special needs children. These mothers have developed very real illnesses and pains that prevent them from engaging in the parenting of their children. She reported that when parents do this, they tend to get even sicker. Mom complains of a migraine when her kid is screaming at the top of his lungs and tells dad to handle it. Dad deals with it, and mom gets out of dealing with the screaming kid. Mom's migraines become more and more frequent. As a behavior analyst, she calls this negative reinforcement. Described by B. F. Skinner in his theory of operant conditioning, negative reinforcement occurs when a behavior is reinforced by removing a negative outcome.[27] (Read between the lines: the neural pathways get stronger.) She even works with parents to reframe and diffuse these situations. Essentially, she is uncrossing the tangled wires.

These cross-wired emotions get stronger over time. Any time you've ever gotten sick for attention, or angry for motivation, or depressed for love, you built a pattern in the neural network of your brain. You unintentionally and unconsciously buddied those emotions up. You need a surge of energy to complete a project, so you manifest anger to get you there. When that pattern runs the same circuits over and over and over again, it creates an automatic program. Soon enough, every time you need a surge of energy, you generate anger or manifest circumstances in your life that will make you angry.

There's a secondary gain that comes with those negative emotions. They may feel heavy, they may have even changed the course of your life, but by experiencing them you have learned some interesting things about yourself. There were some positive outcomes, shifts or changes that came as a result. If you examine these situations closely, you'll find that there is some sort of secondary gain there as well, so you continue to rerun the patterns. The more it happens, the stronger this circuitry becomes. It traps the energy. It keeps you limited to that particular pattern, and that particular circuitry. It robs you of your energy because you're giving energy away to the program. Even though it seems like you're getting spurts of energy from playing out the program, the truth is that these programs deplete you of your energy. They keep you trapped in an endless cycle of repeating the pattern, until the pain of continuing to repeat the pattern exceeds the pain of staying stuck.

Sure, there's secondary gain. But it's not lasting energy. It may give you a rush to fight with your partner and you enjoy the secondary gain of connecting when you make up, but it uses far too much energy. Staying stuck in the program limits your choices. It robs you of true freedom. Your energy is so entangled in the pattern, you can't use your creativity. You have no energy to manifest, or to heal yourself. You're a slave to the pattern. Your experience becomes limited to the program.

The stronger your cross-wired emotions become as a buddies, the harder it is to build new neural pathways in the brain. Those buddied emotions are codependent. They're terrified of doing anything alone, especially if they've been buddies for a long time, or if their relationship has been an intense one. By the way, the emotional buddy pattern in your neural circuitry is the exact same pattern that's in your DNA. Double whammy.

It takes courage to break the patterns. You have to really want to shift. You must get real with your emotions. You have to be willing to look at your emotions, and excavate them layer by layer. You can't be so afraid that you don't admit them to yourself. Know that your head is going to try to protect you from the pattern. That's why it's so important to stay in your heart.

Pattern-busting is hard, but not impossible. Thanks to your brain's amazing ability to rewire itself, there is hope that you will break free from the pattern and learn to create new circuitry. Rick Hanson, Ph.D., a neuropsychologist and author of the books *Hardwiring Happiness* and *Buddha's Brain*, discusses the mind and brain as a unified system. They are in a circular relationship with each other. He writes in his article "Mind Changing Brain Changing Mind: The Dharma and Neuroscience," "The integration of mind and brain has three important implications. First, as your brain changes, your mind changes. Second, as your mind changes, your brain changes. Many of these changes are fleeting, as your brain changes moment to moment to support the movement of information. But many are lasting, as neurons wire together: structure builds in the brain."[28]

Doing the HEAL Technique® brings these subconscious programs up into the conscious mind. That is the beginning of the shift– catching those wayward cross-wired programs red handed! Bringing the subconscious pattern to the surface so your conscious mind can become aware is the very first step.

Energy never dies. We learned this in elementary school science as the first law of thermodynamics, the law of conservation of energy. Energy cannot be created or destroyed. It just changes form, which means you can always reclaim the energy you've given away to these ornery little programs you've been running. The energy never goes so far away from you that you can't get it back. We can change the way we react, respond, create and experience the world around us just by creating subtle shifts. We can decondition and reprogram ourselves. We have the power to change the way we experience everything that we feel is not serving us in a positive way. The more we shift, the more we are creating new circuitry, thanks to neuroplasticity.

As you clear patterns, you'll become more and more aware of them in your life. You'll be more conscious of them. Just bringing them into your field of awareness will help shift it, because they can no longer hide out in the shadows of the subconscious.

It's actually quite simple to get there. Believe it or not, you're only a HEAL session and a few short breaths away from a real shift.

10) YOU ARE THE BREATH: *Breathing From Your Heart*

Breath is life force. It is so integral to life, delivering oxygen to every cell in your body, every moment of your life. But it happens so automatically that most of us take it for granted. For most of us, breathing is an unconscious process. Our bodies breathe in oxygen all day and night, every day and night. We hardly give it a thought. It just happens, typically with shallow breaths. Without oxygen, there is no life. Hand in hand with the heart, breathing is how our organs receive oxygen to sustain life.

Breath impacts everything, instantaneously. Our ability to breathe is a miracle that works through our being with each life-giving inhale and purifying exhale. Breath is our link to awareness and transformation. The more consciousness we bring to our breath, the more we can deepen it and follow our breath back into the center of ourselves. A few deep breaths allow you to pause before reacting out of fear or ego. It gives you a chance to slow down so you don't react from your programming or conditioning. It allows you to take a moment so that you can make a conscious choice out of love. The breath can be a tool to return to your own heart, or to the present moment. You can even ride the breath to expanded states of consciousness. The Chinese call it qi. The Japanese call it ki. Yogis call it prana. "It" is the primordial energy that permeates everything. Breath work is the key to harnessing this life force energy within our own being.

Shallow breathing arises when we suppress our emotions. It's all subconscious, but it can really limit us. It creates tension in our bodies, it makes us feel anxious, and it makes our hearts beat rapidly. This is a self-perpetuating cycle. Short shallow breaths cause all of these not-so-fun side effects, and then those not-so-fun side effects can cause continued shallow breathing.

Anxiety activates your fight or flight response. Your heartbeat accelerates and so does your breathing, increasing oxygen and blood supply to prepare your body to fight or flee. This was great when ancient man had to flee from a hungry lion. Not so great for responding to the bulk of your modern everyday stressors.

Conscious, connected breathing allows your lungs to talk to your brain via the intelligence of your heart. Remember that the heart and the brain are directly connected and the communication that takes place between them is a two-way dialog. We used to think the brain was the only organ that could send commands to the heart and the rest of the body, but the latest scientific research shows that the heart talks to the brain even more than the brain talks to the heart.[29] The heart talks to the rest of the body, too, but not all body parts can talk directly to the brain. Your lungs, for example, don't have a direct line of communication to your brain. Your lungs have to go through a middleman– your heart. So when you're all hopped up on adrenaline after a fight or flight freakout, the only way to tell your brain that you're ok is through the breath. Slow, conscious breathing slows your heart rate, and your lungs are able to tell your heart, "It's cool– we're ok." The heart, in turn, tells the brain all is well. No need to release cortisol. It's all good.

Conscious heart-centered breath work also influences your electromagnetic field. How could it not? Your heart's electromagnetic field is massive. Slow, deep breaths bring the heart into coherence. This is when the heartbeat moves into a stable, consistent rhythmic pattern. Dr. Rollin McCraty, Research Director at the Institute of HeartMath, explained coherence as "the state when the heart, mind and emotions are in energetic alignment and cooperation. It is a state that builds resiliency– personal energy is accumulated, not wasted–leaving more energy to manifest intentions and harmonious outcomes."[30] When your heart is in a state of coherence, it affects everything else in your vibrational field, causing dense, lower vibrational patterns to transform into higher vibrational energy. Through the intentional process of heart-centered breath work, old patterns can be cleared and restructured.

Breathing is the most natural, organic path to your heart. Your breath regulates your heart. Focusing on your breath–which is so easy to do once you bring conscious awareness to it–gives you direct access to your heart. Deep, slow, steady breathing brings your heart into a balanced rhythmic rate. Remember, your heart is your most powerful electromagnetic field and informs the universe at large. Breathing consciously and intentionally gives you the opportunity to set intentions within your heart, and to make choices out of love.

BREATH, YOUR BRAINWAVES, AND YOUR STATES OF BEING

Remember that every experience you've had and every emotion you've felt gets recorded and stored in your body by means of your brainwaves. Your brainwave state at any time that you experience a highly charged emotional event determines how and where that charge will be stored within your being. It provides the first insight into your personal healing codes.

Through heart-centered breath work, you can gain access to these stored emotional patterns, brainwave frequencies and memories. Your breath is the means by which you can access your heart– your power center. You can also utilize specific breath sequences to impact and recode information within the brainwaves to free stuck energy, let go of dumb-dumb beliefs and liberate patterns that hold you back. You can find out what brainwave state or states that energy is stuck in through muscle testing or any other method for calibrating vibration covered in chapter six, *YOU ARE VIBRATING: Measuring your Vibrations* (p. 63). Here's how certain breath sequences correspond to your brainwave states:

BETA
Find release in the beta brainwave state with a mouth-mouth (MM) breath. The mouth-mouth breath is coded to let go of negative emotions, stuck energy, trauma, pain and cross-wired emotions on the physical level. This breath helps relieve tension, reduces stress, aids in detoxification, strengthens your immune system, improves circulation, increases energy in the physical body, and is also very grounding.

ALPHA
Use a mouth-nose (MN) breath to breathe out charges lodged in the alpha brainwave state. This breath programs the alpha brainwave frequency to

dig out charges and stuck energy in the emotional body. This breath assists in integrating repressed emotions and patterns, liberating you to experience new levels of love and joy.

THETA

Code the breath to get into the theta brainwave state and mental body by doing a nose-nose (NN) breath. This type of breath helps you to clear the subconscious mind, dissolve limiting beliefs, and gain mental clarity. Clearing out charges in theta leads to peace, insight and creativity.

DELTA

Clear energetic blocks in the delta brainwave state by doing a nose-mouth (NM) breath. This breath is coded to clear you on a spiritual level. With nose-mouth breath work, you gain access to higher states of consciousness. Clearing in the delta frequency heightens your awareness of your connection to Source and your connection to everything. This can bring insight and great clarity to life.

GAMMA AND THE THIRTEEN BREATHS

Once you uncover what brainwave states your stagnant energy is caught in, you'll do the corresponding breath work for that brain frequency. It just takes thirteen breaths for each code. Breath work has instantaneous results.

Sometimes you will find that the pattern is caught in multiple brainwaves. That's ok. That actually makes sense. Remember, if it's showing up in the physical (beta), it's really, really, really dense. Physical reality is the most dense– the lowest, slowest vibrational frequency. Before your pattern got so dense that it could actually show up in your physical reality, it likely had to move through the less dense layers of your multi-dimensional being first.

Before it was physical, it may have been emotional (alpha). You may have had so much emotional stuff going on that the pattern condensed and then, BAM! It showed up in your physical body. Before it was emotional, it may have been a thought (theta). Perhaps it was an unconscious or subconscious thought, but stuck energy in the mental layer of your being all the same. Before it was a thought, it was a belief. It existed in the spiritual layer of your being (delta), the lightest, fastest, highest vibrational frequency other than gamma.

When you uncover that your pattern is present in multiple brainwave states, progress through the corresponding breath work by moving from the lightest, fastest vibrations to the densest, slowest vibrations. Begin on the spiritual (delta) end of the spectrum, working your way towards the physical (beta). Your breath work will move in this direction:

Delta	Spiritual	Nose-Mouth
Theta	Mental	Nose-Nose
Alpha	Emotional	Mouth-Nose
Beta	Physical	Mouth-Mouth

For example, if you find that your pattern is stuck in the beta and theta brainwave states, begin with the corresponding theta release breath– a nose-nose breath. Then progress to the beta release breath, mouth-mouth. If you don't know what brainwave state the pattern is jamming up in, don't worry about it. It really doesn't matter. Do all four breaths, beginning with delta and ending with beta, and you're covered. You can't go wrong. The process of discovery is helpful to provide your conscious mind with understanding. This gives you the opportunity to think through and analyze the core of your issues and patterns. You get the opportunity to consciously process these new insights. This isn't necessary at an energetic level. It can all be breathed away by going through the four cycles of breath.

Before you begin the breath work, take a moment to focus your attention on your heart. It helps to tap on your sternum with your fingertips in a gentle thumping motion. Not only does this guide you to keep your awareness on your heart center, but tapping is an emotional version of acupuncture, and tapping your thymus–which is right beneath the sternum–stimulates this energy meridian point similar to the way an acupuncture needle might. Stimulating the thymus gland increases energy levels and opens up the heart. On a side note, thymus thumping also creates vibrations and stimulates the thymus to produce T-cells, which boost immune system function. The vibrations caused by tapping draw blood and energy into the thymus. Try it. Notice how it stimulates your energy system, awakens the heart and lungs, and gives you a sense of strength and vitality. All are helpful for shifting and transforming.

When you inhale, imagine that you're breathing deep into your heart. Take deep, exaggerated breaths, filling completely from the bottom up to the top of the lungs. Imagine the oxygen moving through you, encoding you with new information– the frequency of love. When you exhale, imagine that you are breathing out through your heart. Exaggerate the outbreath, expelling all of the air fully from your lungs. Imagine the exhale purifying you, moving stuck energy through your being as well as oxygen from your lungs.

Repeat this pattern of deep, exaggerated inhales and exhales for twelve breaths. The number twelve represents a completed cycle of experience. With the thirteenth inhale, once you fill up your lungs fully and completely, hold the breath for as long as you can. Feel the oxygen swirl through you, sending you into a gamma brainwave state. The number thirteen is the doorway to a higher level of consciousness. The thirteenth breath is the doorway to transformation– the end of something old and a rebirth. With this thirteenth breath, you generate gamma and recode the old information, birthing something new: Increased consciousness. Increased energy. Healing. A higher vibration. The frequency of unconditional love.

Sighs and yawns are a good sign. Yawning brings in serious O_2, which raises the vibration. I bet you're yawning right now, aren't you? When you're tired and trying to keep awake, you yawn. It brings in oxygen and raises your alertness, bringing you back into beta. When you're waking up in the morning and you're transitioning brainwave states, you yawn. You need oxygen to process the clearing and healing, too. Yawning rocks.

Oh, and you get high, too. One hundred percent natural and organic.

11) YOU ARE RENEWING: *Reclaiming Your Energy*

Candace was concerned about her brother. Three months earlier, she was grateful and relieved when Zane came home after his third tour in Iraq. She had spent the last few years worrying about him constantly. She thought her anxieties would be over when he was finally back at home, but she was more concerned than ever now.

He wasn't sleeping much. He was always on edge. She could hear him screaming in his sleep in the middle of the night, almost every night. She knew he was having nightmares. When she tried to talk to him about it, he would shut down.

He had only planned to stay with her for a few weeks until he could find an apartment and get settled back into civilian life, but in the three months that Zane had been home, he hadn't really left the house. He made no attempts to find a place to live or to find a job. He wasn't even making an effort to get out of his pajamas or brush his teeth. Candace was trying to give him space. She didn't want to rush him. She wanted to allow him to integrate back into his old life in his own time.

That is, until now. Candace woke up at 4:30 a.m. for a business trip. She thought it was strange that the light was on in Zane's room and music was playing. She felt a sense of foreboding wash over her. She knocked lightly on the door, not wanting to startle him. There was no answer. She knocked a little more forcefully. Still no answer.

Candace pushed the door open. Zane lay on the bed, his eyes open but vacant. A chill rushed down her spine as she raced over to his side. He was breathing... but barely. She placed her fingers on his neck and felt a very faint pulse. She called 911 immediately and paramedics were on the scene in a matter of minutes. Candace cancelled her business trip and rode along to the hospital in the ambulance with her younger brother.

At the hospital, Zane's stomach was pumped and doctors were able to stabilize him. He had taken thirty sleeping pills that his doctor had prescribed for insomnia. After being held at the hospital for three days of observation, Zane was released. Candace felt scared and helpless. Not knowing how to help her brother, she made an appointment with Carolanne and begged him to go. He reluctantly agreed.

"What is it that you would like to shift today, Zane?" Carolanne asked at the beginning of the session. She was aware of his suicide attempt, but wanted Zane to set the intention for the session.

"I want the nightmares to stop. I want to stop re-experiencing what went on over there. I just want to be free from it all. I just want to live a normal life," Zane told her, articulating his feelings for the first time.

"Ok, let me just get a little bit of information from your body." Carolanne muscle tested Zane to get his starting vibration: zero and ninety. Fear and rage. She proceeded to muscle test him to get a range of data and learned that zero percent of his soul was in his body, his self-love was at zero percent and he was only ready for his organic life path by fifty percent. She also uncovered that the trauma was in all four brainwave states. His struggle was physical, emotional, mental and spiritual. They would be doing a lot of breath work that day.

"Feel into your nightmares. Feel into your memories of being in combat in Iraq, and what it's like to re-experience that now that you are back home. How does it make you *feel*?" Carolanne prompted.

"I feel like I'm in danger," Zane explained.

"What's the feeling of being in danger?" Carolanne prodded. Danger wasn't an emotion. She wanted him to feel the emotion.

"I'm terrified," Zane muttered quietly.

"What's the intensity of that feeling on a scale of zero to ten, with ten being the highest?" Carolanne asked.

"It's a ten," he answered without a moment's hesitation.

"When you feel into being terrified, how does that make you feel?" Carolanne dug deeper.

"Panicked," Zane answered.

"What's the intensity, zero to ten?"

"A ten."

"Now peel back the feelings of panic. What's underneath?" Carolanne continued in this process of digging up layer after layer of energy and emotion.

"I feel stuck. It's debilitating."

"What's the intensity, zero to ten?"

"Ten again."

"What's under the feeling of being stuck and debilitated?"

"Anger. I'm angry. I'm pissed."

"Good," Carolanne continued. "Feel into that anger. What's the intensity?"

"Ten."

"When you feel angry, how does that make you feel?"

"Like I'm on high alert," Zane answered.

"What does being on high alert feel like?" Carolanne redirected him back to his emotions.

"Anxious."

"How do you rate the intensity of that anxiety?"

"Ten."

"What's underneath your feelings of anxiety?"

"I don't know," Zane answered. His eyes looked empty and his voice sounded hollow.

"Close your eyes and put your hands on your heart," Carolanne directed him. "Feel into that anxiety. How does it make you feel?"

"Exhausted. It makes me feel exhausted. And drained. And depleted."

"Goooooooood," Carolanned cooed reassuringly. "Now feel into it. How would you rate the intensity of being exhausted, drained and depleted?"

"Ten."

"What's the feeling underneath this exhaustion and depletion?"

"Numb. I don't feel anything."

"How would you rate it?"

"Five," Zane answered listlessly.

"When you feel into that feeling of numbness, how does that make you feel?" Carolanne continued.

"Guilty. I'm alive and some of my friends weren't so lucky. So I feel guilty. For being alive. For wasting this second chance at life. I just feel guilty." His voice began to crack but his face showed no emotion.

"What's the intensity of your guilt?"

"Umm… also a ten," he answered.

"When you feel guilty, how does that make you feel?"

"Terrified." His eyes met Carolanne's. He had come full circle back to the first emotion in the pattern. Guilt was at the root of the emotional pattern. He was giving away massive amounts of energy to this pattern and guilt was at the root of holding the pattern in place, siphoning off his life force energy.

"Excellent work, Zane," Carolanne encouraged. "Go ahead and keep your hands on your heart with your eyes closed. I want you to feel into your feelings of guilt. Where in your body are you storing these feelings?"

"Everywhere," Zane answered.

"Where specifically?" Carolanne nudged.

Zane took a deep breath and placed his awareness in his physical body. Then he was able to be more specific about where the feelings of guilt resided.

"In my chest as a tightness and in my throat as a choking feeling. I feel it in my stomach– it always feels like it's in knots. I feel it in my arms and legs as anxiety. I feel it in my head like a terrible pressure. But mostly I feel it in my heart. My heart is breaking."

"Wow, Zane. Very good. Now I want you to tell me the first time you felt that guilt. I'm going to count backwards from five to one and I want you to tell me the first memory that pops up for you. Five… four… three… two… one. Drop into that memory. When did you first feel this emotion of guilt?"

"My squad was on patrol in Baghdad and this kid walks up," Zane began to recall. His voice sounded distant. "He couldn't have been much older than twelve. I wasn't too close, so I couldn't see all that much but I do remember a palpable feeling of fear. Then I hear yelling. All the guys around me are yelling. They are all saying to shoot the kid, but no one does. Then I saw that he was wearing a suicide vest. It was just total chaos. I don't know what happened next, but there was an explosion. I felt the heat. My buddy is screaming and his clothes are burning right off of him. Then there's shots being fired everywhere. Firing all around me. And everyone is dead. They're all just on the ground, dead and dying."

"What is the intensity of that memory, zero to ten?" Carolanne asked, her voice quavering. Zane's story had visibly moved her.

"On a scale of zero to ten, probably a hundred," he answered, his voice still distant. "It's intense."

"Of course it is," Carolanne reassured. "I know it was traumatic and intense and so painful. But you're here. You survived. You're alive. So through the whole process, what good things did you learn about yourself?"

"I don't know," Zane said.

"Pretend you do know. What were some of the positive outcomes of this experience?" Carolanne probed deeper.

"I guess I learned that I am resilient."

"OK, good. And how does it make you feel to realize that you are resilient?" She was digging again.

"It makes me feel strong."

"What does feeling strong feel like?"

"I feel hopeful."

"And when you feel hopeful, what do you feel?"

"When I feel hopeful, I feel renewed."

"What does feeling renewed feel like for you?"

"It feels very calm."

"When you feel calm, how do you feel?"

"Happy."

"And when you feel happy, what do you feel?"

"I feel peace."

"And what does peace feel like for you?"

"It feels like joy."

"Amazing work, Zane. You really dug deep. And you just uncovered an important subconscious pattern that you've been giving all of your energy away to. Now we have your codes. Are you ready to hear it?" Carolanne asked thoughtfully.

Zane nodded. He was ready.

Carolanne began to muscle test each of the cross-wired emotions:

"Feeling terrified leads to feeling resilient." Zane's muscles held strong for truth.

"In order to feel strong, you must first experience panic." He held firm still.

"In order to feel hopeful, you much first feel stuck and debilitated." True again.

"Anger leads to feeling renewed." Also true.

"In order to feel calm, you must first feel anxious." His muscles held strong again. Truth.

"Feeling exhausted, drained and depleted leads to feeling happy." Also true.

"In order to feel peace, you must first be numb." True. Very interesting.

"Feelings of guilt lead to feelings of joy." Truth again.

His muscles held strong, telling both Carolanne and Zane that there was a serious issue with cross-wired emotions in his subconscious.

"So, Zane, what you've told me through this process is that you have a pattern of creating certain heavy emotions in order to be able to experience another set of light, positive emotions. The light, positive emotions aren't necessarily related to each other, but your brain has linked them together. You've been giving away your energy to this pattern. That means that holding this pattern of creating feelings of being terrified, panicked, stuck and debilitated, angry, anxious, exhausted, drained and depleted, numb and guilty is draining your energy. How would you like to reclaim all of the energy you have given away to this pattern?"

"I would love nothing more," Zane answered.

"Wonderful," Carolanne continued. "And how would you like to be able to experience resilience, strength, hope, renewal, calmness, happiness, peace and joy from the vibration of unconditional love instead of giving your energy away to the pattern?"

"I would love to," he responded with a new sense of anticipation.

Carolanne and Zane continued to do the breath work in all four brainwave states in order to clear the pattern and open up the flow of energy.

Carolanne's latest update from Candace and Zane was promising. Zane's nightmares have diminished in frequency and intensity. Every now and then he has a nightmare, but they are not as debilitating as they were before. Zane reported that he has found closure as a part of his healing. He was finally able to cry and experience his grief. He has visited the graves of his fallen comrades to say goodbye and even visited some of their families. He is speaking out about his experiences in Iraq and honoring the memory of his friends. He has found purpose in his life again because he was able to reclaim the energy that he was giving away to post-traumatic stress, anxiety and reliving the trauma and devastation of war repeatedly in his nightmares.

RECLAIMING ENERGY

You are an unlimited spiritual being with infinite power and limitless potential, condensed down into itty-bitty human form. Energetically, you're huge. But in your physical body, you have a finite amount of energy. In fact, that's exactly why we need sleep. We sleep at night so that we can replenish our physical energy and process the experiences of our day.

Pretend your energy allotment for the day is represented by a set of gold coins. Let's say you get a stack of ten gold coins for the day. That's your daily energy allocation. It takes five or six of those gold coins to run the daily functions of your body– controlling your blood pressure, making your heart beat, breathing, regulating your body temperature, balancing water and electrolytes, regulating your metabolism and digesting your food. It takes another gold coin or two for physical activities and daily movement– getting out of bed, brushing your teeth, going to work, going about your day, exercising and performing any other movement. That leaves you with two to four gold coins of energy each day to be creative, express yourself, manifest your desires, or live your life's dream.

What most people don't realize is that subconscious programs consume a lot of those remaining few coins of your body's daily energy allotment. It takes a lot of energy to bury emotions and keep them buried. There isn't much left over to live your highest vision for your life when your energy is being used up by running subconscious programs. It's like having too many windows open on your computer. You're running email, Google, ten Microsoft Word documents, a few Excel files, Powerpoint, Facebook, and Instagram. You've forgotten about the other programs running in the background and your Google search results are taking forever. All of your subconscious memories and programs are the same, eating away at your capacity and performance bit by bit, all below the level of conscious awareness. It's no wonder you sometimes get run down and your body crashes. It's no wonder you have no energy left over to start your dream business, or attract your soul mate, or kick cancer to the curb.

Every experience and memory you have ever had has been imprinted on your subconscious. Everything is stored there. Always. It's like your body's computer storage system. Those memories either have a positive charge, a negative charge or they are neutral. Some have bigger, stronger charges, like the death of a loved one. These eat up more storage space– more memory. The death of a child might eat up the cellular equivalent of a terabyte of data. And you still have all kinds of other miscellaneous minor charges taking up space– a megabyte here, a gigabyte there, like the bully from second grade that pushed you on the playground, or the fight with your dad when he called you a loser.

Energy is energy. It can't be created or destroyed. It simply changes form. If you've given away your energy to heavy emotions and subconscious patterns that don't serve your highest good and your organic life purpose, you can reclaim that energy at any time. Your lost energy is never so far away from you that you can't get it back.

PLUG THE LEAKS

Before you can begin reclaiming the energy you have leaked, it makes sense to plug the leaks. This means finding the subconscious programs you're running that cause you to leak energy. Learn to recognize what drains your energy. What makes you feel depleted? Look at toxic life situations, toxic people in your life, and habitual patterns of behavior like anxiety, procrastination or guilt. They all greedily eat up your daily energy budget of gold coins. And they're always hungry for more, those insatiable little buggers.

What is it that you would like to shift in your life? How is not shifting that situation depleting you? As you go through the process of using the HEAL Technique® to pinpoint life events that triggered the programs that rob you of your energy, pay attention to the heavy, negative emotions. Tune in to how they make you feel in your body. As you uncover the light, positive emotions that got cross-wired, notice the hidden belief systems that have kept that energy-stealing pattern in place. Notice how high-intensity charges may have triggered a pattern and consider how you may be leaking energy to that pattern. Contemplate how you may have consistently given energy away to this pattern throughout your life.

Awareness is key. Once you have awareness, you bring the subconscious elements of your life into conscious focus– you bring consciousness to what was previously controlling and depleting you. You're essentially getting out of your own way and putting your higher self into the driver's seat of your life.

When you neutralize the charges, you dissolve the power that holds that pattern in place. You're able to shift into a new awareness and think in a whole new way. That shift into a higher consciousness allows you to reclaim the energy that you have given away so you have more energy available to you. Through shifting, you're able to reclaim all the energy you've leaked. Not only that, you're able to plug the leaks so you never have to leak energy that way again.

From that space of awareness, you are able to take different actions and make different decisions in alignment with your highest vision for yourself, instead of being a slave to your subconscious programming. From that space of elevated consciousness, you may choose to eliminate toxic relationships, contaminated life situations, and destructive behavior from your life. From that space of heightened awareness, you move through your life in a way that allows you to avoid–or at least minimize– the energy seepage, and you will finally be able to reclaim lost energy.

FILL YOUR TANK

Once you stop the outflow of energy and plug up the leaks, you can identify what fills your tank– what gives you more gold coins of energy: prayer, meditation, spiritual practices, self-expression, healthy relationships, pleasure, fulfillment, adventure, play, purpose and fun. Just like food nourishes the physical body and provides you with one form of energy, filling your tank nourishes your soul and provides an entirely different, but still essential, type of energy. Joshua Rosenthal, founder and director of the Institute of Integrative Nutrition, calls this primary food. He says, "Sometimes we are not fed by food but by the energy of our lives. These moments and feelings demonstrate that everything is food. We take in thousands of experiences of life that can fulfill us physically, mentally, emotionally and spiritually."[31] So make it a point to do things in your life that feed your soul.

Filling your tank is not selfish. When you're on an airplane, flight attendants instruct you to secure your oxygen mask first, before helping others. You'll do no one any good if you've passed out from lack of oxygen. Taking care of yourself is generous. When you fill yourself up first, you have more to offer and more to give. If you don't fill your own tank first, you won't have anything left over to give or share with others.

You have to plug the leaks first. If the integrity of your energy field is compromised, then your attempts to fill your tank will be futile. Plug up that leakage and reclaim all of the energy you've given away to people, belief systems, programming, and situations that have sucked the life out of you.

Reclaiming your energy renews you and allows you to reclaim your power. Reclaiming your personal power is a vital and essential ingredient in living in alignment with your organic truth. Reclaiming your power is a spiritual experience– a personal experience of the divine. It's the experience of feeling loved unconditionally, so much so that it overflows. You are so filled with love that you can't help but love others unconditionally.

So stop the leaks, reclaim your energy and fill your tank. That's what the shift is all about. Your own shift will have far-reaching effects. Your energetic frequency impacts all aspects of your life and far beyond. You are more powerful than you can imagine.

12) YOU ARE TRANSFORMING: *Making the Shift*

Completing the process of the HEAL Technique® is transformative. You're making an energetic upgrade, shifting out of an old lower vibration into a new higher vibration. In order to make the shift, it's important to have a willingness to release old patterns. Letting go of old conditioned patterns, belief systems and wounds and reclaiming the energy you have given away to those traumas brings expanded awareness and renewed energy in order to shift, transform and create something new in your life.

After a healing session, you will go through a period of integration and rebalancing. Everyone experiences energy healing differently. We are all unique. We each have our own exclusive energetic signature and unique healing codes. After completing the process of the HEAL Technique®, take notice of what feels different for you. The work doesn't stop when you complete the HEAL Technique®. Healing continues after the session. You will continue to shift, integrate and process the healing after the session. You'll continue to have revelations beyond the session, too.

When most people first complete the process of the HEAL Technique®, they immediately report feeling lighter, like a weight has been lifted. Most of the time, people experience a heightened sense of energy and a general feeling of well-being. You can expect a feeling of being unburdened by old patterns that have kept you feeling stuck. This typically leads to feeling a sense of empowerment. You may also feel more focused, have greater clarity, feel more excited about life, and be more motivated. The intense charges associated with the pain of traumatic experiences in your past are neutralized, releasing their stranglehold on you. There is often also a knowingness– a feeling of being "done with it." Old patterns are being torn down and you're building new neural pathways in your brain. You're laying the foundation to create new experiences in your life.

It's similar to strength training. When you lift weights, you create tiny tears in the fiber and connective tissue of your muscles. It makes you feel sore– sometimes after a really grueling workout it can be pretty painful. But when you nourish your body, rest and repair, your muscles heal, becoming bigger and stronger.

Energy healing is the same. Going through the process of the HEAL Technique® is an energetic workout. It tears down the fibers of old belief systems and unhealthy patterns that no longer serve you. Once old patterns are broken down, you must restore a new, higher vibrational balance. Growth comes from proper nourishment, rest and repair. It typically takes one to three sleep cycles to get enough rest to adequately repair and restore your body's energy balance. Sleep is essential for integration and restoration. Physically, your cells are doing a lot of repairing when you sleep, but sleep repairs your being on all levels– emotionally, mentally and spiritually. Sleep promotes accelerated growth.

Transformative shifts are most often immediate, but it may take one to three days to really integrate and anchor the new energy. Trust the process and know that whatever happens is perfect for you at the time. You may continue to experience shifts after a session for a longer period of time– days, weeks or even months. Often, when you look back you will realize how much in your life actually transformed as a result of a session. Hindsight is always 20/20.

Going through the process of the HEAL Technique® shifts you at the most fundamental levels, changing and rearranging your being at an energetic level. With that kind of reorganization, it may take a couple days to find a new internal balance.

As rebalancing continues and you begin to integrate the healing, you may experience outbursts of suppressed emotion. You may want to laugh hysterically. You may have the urge to weep uncontrollably. After my first session of the HEAL Technique®, I found myself caught off guard because I did both–laughed and cried–simultaneously and unexpectedly. Ride the emotional wave and give yourself the time and space for these feelings to move through you and be released. You're cleansing emotions embedded in the unconscious. It will pass. It's just old baggage coming out of the tissues.

The HEAL Technique® is essentially an energetic detox. As such, you may experience detox symptoms similar to those you experience during a cleanse. You may feel emotionally or physically worse for a few days after a session because the junk is being stirred up in order to clear it out. Cleansing is absolutely necessary for healing.

Some detox or healing symptoms may include: headache, crying, fever (as you burn off old energy), diarrhea (release), dizziness, feeling spaced out, time distortion, fatigue, insomnia, sleepiness, and general aches and pains. You may feel depressed or irritable. You may experience flu-like symptoms as part of the detoxification process as you release old, lower vibrations.

Don't be alarmed. This is a healing reaction. It's a normal part of the healing process. Even though it may feel uncomfortable, a healing reaction is a good sign because it means you are clearing out the old energy and regenerating. You're releasing old patterns and reclaiming lost energy. These symptoms are part of the process. Remember, it is only temporary. These symptoms shouldn't last longer than two or three days. If they do, and you've already tried some of the tips below, I encourage you to reach out to us via the HEAL website, http://healingenergyandlearning.com/contact/. Once you have come through the healing process, your energy will have shifted into a new, higher vibration. You'll see things more clearly, like you've woken up from a deep sleep. Notice what you are receiving through this process. Pay attention to what comes your way.

During this process, be gentle with yourself. For a few days after doing sessions using the HEAL Technique®, prioritize self-care, nurture your spirit, drink a lot of water and get plenty of rest– mentally, physically and emotionally.

Here are some ideas for self-care after a healing session:

1. Drink plenty of water. Water is important to flush out toxins– physically and energetically.
2. Take a warm, soothing, epsom salt bath. Light some candles. Add some lavender oil. Do some deep breathing.

3. Spend some time in nature. Go for a walk outside. Take some deep, cleansing breaths. Walk on the earth with bare feet.

4. Journal. Write as an outlet to sort out your feelings and understand your healing response. Observe the changes in your mind and body. Use your journal to gain personal insights.

5. Pay gentle and compassionate attention to yourself during this healing time. Listen to your body. Give yourself whatever you need.

6. Breathe deeply. Take time to be still and do some deep breathing throughout the day. Relax.

7. Create a ritual of letting go. Write or draw whatever it is that you would like to release and burn it, or offer it to the Earth.

8. Celebrate. Express gratitude. You have birthed yourself anew. Expect miracles.

13) THE HEAL TECHNIQUE®: *Your Doorway to Transformation*

Whatever is going on with you that you would like to shift is energetic at its very source. It doesn't matter if it's physical disease, depression or anxiety, a change in career path, relationship issues, financial concerns, family drama, abuse, addiction, conquering phobias, manifesting abundance, manifesting anything, opening up to creativity, self-worth and self-love, finding your life's purpose, or simply creating more joy in your life. It's all energy. All of your thoughts, emotions, wishes, desires, the things you want to change, shift, heal and transform– all energy. Your energetic frequency impacts everything in your life– the people around you, the circumstances of your life and the reality you experience. A simple shift in your energetic vibration can radically transform your whole life. You have the power to make that shift. Now you have a simple tool to help you do it.

The HEAL Technique® is based on months and months of research, experimentation and fine-tuning. It's been simplified so anyone can do it to experience a profound shift in any area of their life. The HEAL Technique® helps you to discover your unique personal codes to shift, then guides you to dive straight into your energetic blocks and remove them easily and painlessly. It's so simple and so effective. The results are profound. You don't even need a certified practitioner. You don't have to pay anyone else to do it for you. Do it by yourself, for yourself, or do it with a friend. You just have to take responsibility for your energy and trust in the wisdom of your heart.

This is what we've been building up to. Now let's get down to the nuts and bolts of it.

THE HEAL TECHNIQUE® WORKSHEET

Begin by writing your name and dating the top of the HEAL Technique® worksheet (p. 150). Always date it with the month, day and year. Future you will have so much freaking fun revisiting how things shifted in your life because present you took responsibility for your energy. In a HEAL session, you'll focus on one area of your life that you want to shift, but you'll be amazed to see how it has a ripple effect into other facets of your life, and impacts the people in your life as well. Sometimes you have to look at where you've been to appreciate how far you've come, so date the worksheet and your future self will thank you.

Feel into what you'd like to shift. Get out of your head. Get out of your story. To determine what you authentically need to work on, you must decide from your heart. Before you focus on manifesting something in your life, clean up the clutter. Clean up your energy and take responsibility for your energy. Work on yourself first.

Then, write out what you would like to shift. Pick ONE THING. You may have five things you want to change or you may have five thousand. For now, just pick one. Now that you've got this handy little tool in your tool belt, it's tempting to hit it hard and tackle a lifetime's worth of shift-worthy items. Patience, my dear. Be gentle with yourself. Go slow and be intentional. It took you at least one lifetime, probably many, to be exactly where you are today. Honor where you are right now in this very moment. Then pick the one thing in your life that you would like to shift right now. There will be time to get to the rest later. Don't divide your energy. Just for now, bring all of your focus, attention and energy to that one thing. Write it down on your HEAL Technique® worksheet. Be as specific as possible. State it in the positive by focusing on what you want to shift or create. Don't focus on what you don't want. Focus on what you do want. What is the outcome that you desire? Write it down.

Let's use an example to illustrate. Say you want to find your own voice. You're tired of holding back and playing small. You might phrase that as "finding my truth and having the courage to speak it."

What you would like to shift:

_____

_____

CALIBRATING VIBRATIONS

If you jumped straight to the back of the book to dive headfirst into the HEAL Technique® (something we would do!) and you don't know how to calibrate your vibration, then you'll have to go back and read chapter six, *YOU ARE VIBRATING: Measuring your Vibrations* (p. 63). You can pretty much skip everything else. It's all icing on the cake anyway. All good in-depth background information, but not necessary to fill your brain with in order for the HEAL Technique® to work for you.

Before getting started, if you're muscle testing, test for accuracy. If you're tipping, get your "yes" and your "no" first. If you're getting your information by using your intuition, jump on in!

STARTING VIBRATION

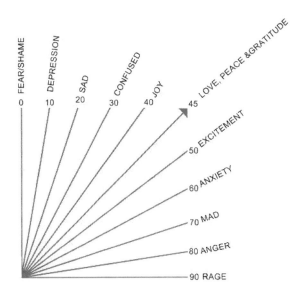

Next, calibrate your starting vibration in reference to what it is that you would like to shift. This is your energetic "before" pic. With starting vibrations, we're looking for two numbers– one number below forty-five and one number above it.

Starting Vibration: _____/_____

When testing your starting vibration, begin with the two outer edges of the right angle in the chart on the previous page–zero and ninety– and work your way in towards the middle until you have your two numbers. You could do this in a couple ways:

Through muscle testing or tipping. State out loud and test, "My starting vibration in reference to _____ is at a zero." Is that true for you?

If so, find your second number (46-90). "My starting vibration is at a 90." Is that true for you? If so, congrats! You've got your two numbers! Fear/shame and rage.

If not, keep testing until you have two numbers– one on either side of neutral (45).

Or simply use your intuition. Tune in to your heart. Say out loud to yourself, "My starting vibration in reference to _____ is at a _____ and _____." Allow your intuition to fill in the blanks. One number between zero and forty-four, one number between forty-six and ninety. Trust your heart and your gut.

If it's not 100% accurate, no biggie. It really doesn't matter that much. It won't affect the healing. You could even skip this step if you wanted to. It's just there because sometimes it helps to see the before and after picture energetically. It's like witnessing a jaw-dropping makeover. Your conscious mind loves this kind of stuff–it just eats it up–but it's not completely necessary. Once you clear the pattern, what's most important is that your ending vibration is at a forty-five–the neutral point–the frequency of love, peace and gratitude.

BODY FULL OF SOUL

This measurement gauges how much of your soul is in your body and fully present, versus how much you are running on autopilot. When you're on autopilot, you're running programs of the mind, putting deeper and deeper grooves into those already well-trodden neural pathways. When your soul is present in your body, you feel light and expansive. Some believe this is the presence of God. Indeed, when a soul is fully and completely in the body, it feels God-like. When you embark on the journey of doing HEAL work, you are calling your soul forward. You are teaching the energy of your soul to be increasingly present in the body. If you're feeling stuck in any area of your life, you're likely stuck in a pattern because your soul is not one hundred percent present in your body. This means your soul is not fully and completely in the driver's seat of your life. It means you're not living from the heart. You can read more about this in chapter five, *YOU ARE HEART CENTERED: Living From the Heart* (p. 45).

Body Full of Soul is measured as a percentage. Here's how to get your measurement:

If you're muscle testing or tipping, say out loud and test, "My body full of soul is at _____." Begin at 100% and work your way down in increments of ten until you test positive for a number.

If you're using your intuition, close your eyes and center yourself. Tune in to your heart. Take a few deep breaths, then say out loud, "My body full of soul is at…" Allow your intuition to fill in the blank with a number between zero and one hundred. Trust it! Again, you could completely skip this calculation. It won't impact your results. We just think it's pretty cool to see the before and after pic. It's compelling to see the energetic makeover.

Write the number down on your HEAL Technique® worksheet. You'll circle back around for the "after" pic later.

Body full of Soul %: _____/_____

SELF-LOVE

This one is pretty self-explanatory. We want your self-love to be at one hundred percent. If your love of self and your level of self-worth is off, this means the patterns or programs that you're stuck in are tampering with your ability to truly and completely love and accept yourself. This level is also measured as a percentage. Here's how to get your self-love measurement:

If you're muscle testing or tipping, say out loud and test, "My self-love is at _____." Begin at 100% and work your way down in increments of ten until you test positive for a number.

If you're using your intuition, close your eyes and center yourself. Tune in to your heart. Take a few deep breaths, then say out loud, "My self-love is at..." Allow your intuition to finish the sentence with a number between zero and one hundred. Trust it! Again, this metric is not completely necessary, but it's fun to see where you are starting out before you begin, and amazing to see how this metric shifts after you go through the process of the HEAL Technique®.

Write the number down on your HEAL Technique® worksheet. We'll come back to it at the end.

Self-Love %: _____ / _____

READY FOR ORGANIC LIFE PATH

This measurement tells you how ready you are to be on your true path in life. It tells you how aligned you are with your purpose– what you truly came here to do, and being who you came here to be. This quality is also measured as a percentage. If you are not at one hundred percent, then the patterns you are stuck in cause you to stay off your path by that number. For example, if you uncover that your readiness for your organic life path is at fifty percent, then the pattern you are about to discover through the HEAL Technique® process has caused you to stay off your true path by fifty percent. That means you're living at only fifty percent of your true potential. Time to reclaim that energy and reclaim your power! Here's how to measure this for yourself:

If you're muscle testing or tipping, say out loud and test, "I am ready for my organic life path at _____." Begin at 100% and work your way down in increments of ten until you test positive for a number.

If you're using your intuition, close your eyes and tune in to your heart. Take a few deep breaths. Imagine breathing into your heart, then say out loud, "I am ready for my organic life path at..." Allow your intuition to fill in the blank with a number between zero and one hundred. Trust it! Again, not necessary, but fun!

Write the number down on your HEAL Technique® worksheet. We'll revisit this one, too.

Ready for Organic Life Path %: _____/_____

SOURCE

Next we'll test for the source of the block or imbalance. Is it yours? Is it someone else's? Is it something else? It's yours if it was created or triggered by childhood trauma or anything else that you have experienced in this lifetime or previous lives. It's someone else if you're picking it up from someone else in your life, like a receiver would pick up a satellite station, or if it's from an ancestor and you've inherited a pattern in your DNA. It's something else if anything else is informing your blueprint that is not part of your organic life path. It could be your environment, the media, the food you eat, your cultural programming, or even other energies. When testing for the source or sources of your block, simply get a yes or no for each: mine, someone else's, and something else. Here are a few ways you might go about this:

If you're muscle testing or tipping, say out loud and test, "This is mine." Is it true? Check it off on your HEAL Technique® worksheet if it is.

Then say, "This is someone else's." True or false? Notate it on your sheet if it's true.

Follow that up with, "This is something else." How did you test? Notate it.

If you're using your intuition, close your eyes and tune in to your heart. Take a few deep breaths. Then say aloud, "This is mine." Do you get a gut-yes or a gut-no? Next say, "This is someone else's." What does your gut tell you? Follow that up with, "This is something else." Just listen to that quiet gut feeling of "yes" or "no" deep within your belly. If all else fails, use your imagination and pretend!

Check off the appropriate slot on your HEAL Technique® worksheet based on what you find here.

Mine _____   Someone Else _____   Something Else _____

BRAINWAVE STATES

The last thing we want to measure is which brainwave state the pattern is caught in. This will tell us what layer of your being it is stuck in, and it will guide the corresponding breath work. For details, reference chapter seven, *YOU ARE FREQUENCIES: Your Brainwave Frequencies* (p. 75). The energy might be stuck in multiple brainwave states, so be sure to test them all:

If you're muscle testing or tipping, say each of the following statements out loud and test them for truth separately:

"This is in a beta brainwave state."

"This is in an alpha brainwave state."

"This is in a theta brainwave state."

"This is in a delta brainwave state."

If you're using your intuition, close your eyes and tune in to your heart. Take a few deep breaths. Feel into each one separately. What does your gut tell you? Do you get a gut-yes or a gut-no? Feel deep into your belly and get a "yes" or "no" for each of the following questions that you ask yourself:

Is this in beta?

Is this in alpha?

Is this in theta?

Is this in delta?

Put checkmarks in the corresponding slots on your HEAL Technique® worksheet and notate the corresponding breath work that you will do near the end of the session. Easy breezy.

Brainwave States:

1. Beta: _____ 2. Alpha: _____ 3. Theta: _____ 4. Delta: _____

    MM   MN   NN   NM

CROSSED WIRES

HEAVY EMOTIONS

Next, we begin the process of uncovering the buried layers of emotions. Each layer takes us deeper into the subconscious patterns and belief systems that keep you stuck. Begin with the heavy emotions. Be careful to stay out of the story. Don't get stuck in the mental chatter. You know that story that you tell yourself? Yeah, that keeps you stuck. Your head is going to try to protect you from the pattern, so it's important to *feel* your way through this and really get in touch with the feelings. The source that feeds the energy to keep you stuck in this pattern is your emotions. Stay with the emotion. It must come through the gut and the heart. It may help to close your eyes and put your hands on your heart. If you skipped to the back of the book to get down to the nitty-gritty but you want more information, read chapter eight *YOU ARE EMOTIONAL: Your Energy in Motion* (p. 85) and chapter nine *YOU ARE CROSS-WIRED: Disentangle From the Program* (p. 91).

It's just super important that you really get real with your emotions. Here's a guide:

Feel into the issue you that you want to shift. When you feel into that situation as it exists in this moment, how does it make you feel? Write it down under "Heavy Emotions" on your HEAL Technique® worksheet. Next, rate the intensity of that emotion on a scale of zero to ten with ten being most intense. Jot that number down in the "starting" column under "Scale 0-10."

Sticking with the example at the beginning of the chapter, you want to find your truth and the courage to speak it. Ask yourself how it makes you feel when you are not in your truth, or when you don't have the courage to speak it. Perhaps, for the purpose of this example, you feel really frustrated, at about a level nine intensity.

Heavy Emotions   Scale 0–10
                                        Start

1. frustration   9

Stay with that first heavy emotion for a moment. Feel into it. How does it make you feel? Notate it on your HEAL Technique® worksheet, along with an intensity rating.

Staying with our example above, you would feel into those feelings of frustration at not being able to speak your truth, then ask yourself how feeling frustrated makes you feel. Maybe you find anger, at a level nine intensity.

Heavy Emotions	Scale 0–10
	Start
1. frustration	9
2. anger	9

Feel into that second layer of emotion. Imagine that you can pick it up and feel what's underneath. What's the feeling if you go one layer deeper? Jot it down, along with your rating of the intensity.

Ask yourself what's underneath the feelings of anger. For the purposes of this example, you'll uncover that you feel trapped or suffocated, at a level eight intensity.

Heavy Emotions	Scale 0–10
	Start
1. frustration	9
2. anger	9
3. trapped/suffocated	8

Stay with that third layer of emotion and really feel into it. How does that make you feel? Write it down. Rate it.

Ask yourself, "When I feel into the feeling of being trapped and suffocated, how does that make me feel?" You notice that it makes you feel sad, intensity ten.

Heavy Emotions	Scale 0–10
	Start
1. frustration	9
2. anger	9
3. trapped/suffocated	8
4. sad	10

Stay with that feeling for a moment and really feel into the sensation of it. Imagine being able to peel back that emotion so you can see what is underneath. Rate the intensity and write it all down on your HEAL Technique® worksheet.

Feel into the sadness for a moment. Pretend that you can peel back that sadness and see what's underneath. What feeling is there?

Continue on in this pattern of uncovering each layer of heavy emotions until you loop back around to the first one, or until you feel that you have uncovered them all.

Notice the last emotion on your list. This is the root. This bottom layer of emotion is the one that feeds all of the other emotions in your pattern.

Heavy Emotions	Scale 0–10
	Start
1. frustration	9
2. anger	9
3. trapped/suffocated	8
4. sad	10
5.	
6.	
7.	
8.	
9.	
10.	

DATA STORAGE

Once you've brought all of the subconscious layers of heavy emotions associated with the issue you want to shift up into your conscious mind and onto the pages of your HEAL Technique® worksheet, and the root emotion has been revealed, we want to find out where this foundational emotion is being stored in the body:

Close your eyes and put your hands on your heart. Feel into the root emotion that anchors all of these heavy emotions. Tune in to your body.

Ask yourself, "Where in my body am I storing this emotion?"

Listen and feel for an answer. It may come as a tightness or feeling of contraction somewhere in your body. It may come as an intuitive nudge from within. You may even hear the answer, or see it appear in your mind's eye. If you're having trouble, just pretend. Use your imagination. However you get the answer, just notice and jot it down.

Where in the body is it stored?

_____

MEMORY ASSOCIATED WITH EMOTIONS

Now you've brought the emotional pattern to consciousness. You've got the root. It's no longer an elusive weight, concealed in the mistiness of the subconscious mind. It's on paper. We know where you've stored it in your body. Next, we want to find the first memory associated with your emotion. This is the event that ignited the pattern within you. It's the thing that first flipped the switch, stored the emotion in your body, and triggered this pattern to show up repeatedly in your life. It's the same pattern that's in your DNA. Once we connect to the original memory, we can then look at the issues related to your current situation and see that the pattern is the same. For more detail, read chapter eight *YOU ARE EMOTIONAL: Your Energy in Motion* (p. 85). Here's the cheat sheet:

First, feel into the root emotion. Really stew in it and feel it for a moment. Ask yourself, "What's the memory of the first time I felt this emotion?"

Close your eyes and count backwards from five to one. When you reach one, a memory will pop into your mind. Counting helps to distract your conscious mind so it doesn't get too involved in finding a story. It keeps the ego busy because the mind has to focus on the numbers. This allows the subconscious mind to retrieve the memory of a time when you first felt this root emotion, without the conscious mind getting in the way.

Find the memory. This memory is the trigger that turned on the pattern. Notate the memory on your HEAL Technique® worksheet.

Rate the intensity of that memory on a scale of one to ten, with ten being the most intense. You'll go back later to check to make sure it's been neutralized.

Memory Associated with Emotions:

_____

_____

_____

Starting Intensity   0-10 _____

LIGHT POSITIVE OUTCOMES

Once you've got the associated memory, you want to uncover where your wires are crossed. One way to do this is by asking what good things you have learned about yourself through this experience or memory related to the issue. This helps you to uncover any secondary gains hidden beneath the surface.

Ask yourself, "What good things did I learn about myself?"

Keeping with our example above, I would ask myself what positive things I have learned about myself when I don't speak my truth. Perhaps I uncover that I am compassionate. I worry about the feelings of others and how my truth might hurt them.

Heavy Emotions	Scale 0–10		Light Emotions
	Start	Finish	
1. frustration	9	_____	compassion

Next, dig through the positive, light emotions layer by layer by asking questions like the ones listed in the example below:

Still working with the same example, I would ask, how does it feel when I feel compassionate? Perhaps I realize that I feel relaxed.

I would continue: when I feel relaxed, what do I feel? Maybe I would uncover feeling liberated.

I would continue: what does liberated feel like to me? I might realize that liberated feels happy to me.

| Heavy Emotions | Scale 0–10 | | Light Emotions |
	Start	Finish	
1. frustration	9	_____	compassion
2. anger	9	_____	relaxation
3. trapped/suffocated	8	_____	liberation
4. sad	10	_____	happiness

TEST WHERE YOUR WIRES ARE CROSSED

Once you've peeled back the layers of the heavy emotions and uncovered the light, positive emotions, it's time to test to find out which ones are crossed. **Don't skip this step.** Your brain needs to see this. Taking the time to test where you created associations between unrelated emotions in your brain is what brings this pattern up into the conscious mind. Bringing it to the surface of your conscious awareness will help you to recognize where else in your life this pattern is showing up. The stronger the intensity, the more tightly the cross-wired emotions are entangled. Awareness changes everything. The patterns can no longer hide in the shadows. Your brain has plasticity. You can rewire it, just by becoming conscious of the subconscious patterns that keep you stuck. You can read chapter nine *YOU ARE CROSS-WIRED: Disentangle from the Program* (p. 91) for more details. Let's test where you've buddied up unrelated emotions and gotten your wires crossed. Here's how:

First, look at the pattern of layered heavy emotions. Then, look at the pattern of light, positive emotions. Simply sit with this information for a moment. This was what your subconscious mind revealed.

If you're muscle testing, check to test for accuracy. If you're tipping, get your "yes" and your "no."

Next, take the first emotion on the Heavy Emotions side of the list and test to see if you've linked it with the first emotion on the Light side of the list. Continue to work your way down the list until you've tested for cross-references between each heavy emotion and the corresponding light emotion.

Sticking with our working example of wanting to shift into having the courage to speak our truth, our HEAL Technique® worksheet would look like this:

Heavy Emotions	Scale 0–10		Light Emotions
	Start	Finish	
1. frustration	9	_____	compassion
2. anger	9	_____	relaxation
3. trapped/suffocated	8	_____	liberation
4. sad	10	_____	happiness

To test if frustration is cross-wired with compassion, you might say, "In order to feel compassionate, I must first feel frustrated." Test for truth.

To test if anger is cross-wired with feeling relaxed, you might say, "To get to feelings of relaxation, I must first go through feelings of anger." Is this true?

To test if feelings of being trapped and suffocated are cross-wired with feeling liberated, you might say, "Feeling trapped and suffocated leads to feeling liberated." Yes or no?

To test if feeling sad is cross-wired with feeling happy, you might say, "In order to feel happy, I must first feel sad." True or untrue?

If any of the above tests as untrue, continue testing to see what emotions on the heavy side are cross-wired with emotions on the light side. You will find they are cross-linked. Use your intuition to guide you. Notate the cross-references.

Contemplate what you have just uncovered. Allow your conscious mind to process this new information. Bring into your awareness and understanding of how you may have seen this pattern at work in your life.

Imagine how it would feel to untangle the energy between these connections so that you can experience the light, positive emotions without having to experience the emotions on the heavy side of the list. Imagine experiencing the light, positive emotions from the energy of love, peace and gratitude instead.

Heavy Emotions	Scale 0–10		Light Emotions
	Start	Finish	
1._____	_____	_____	_____
2._____	_____	_____	_____
3._____	_____	_____	_____
4._____	_____	_____	_____
5._____	_____	_____	_____
6._____	_____	_____	_____
7._____	_____	_____	_____
8._____	_____	_____	_____
9._____	_____	_____	_____
10._____	_____	_____	_____

THE HEAL TECHNIQUE®

Now you've got all of your unique codes to transform, so let's get down to it:

1. First, notice the order of the breath work based on your brainwave states. Work backwards from four to one, moving from the lightest, fastest brainwave frequency to the densest and slowest. Make a note of it.

4) NM _____ 3) NN _____ 2) MN _____ 1) MM _____

2. Next, set your intention out loud. You can use the one provided on the HEAL Technique® worksheet (see below) or make up your own.

I set the intention to eliminate the pattern in all layers, all levels, and all combinations. I also set the intention to neutralize the memories that ignited this pattern. I set the intention to reclaim all of the energy that's been leaked by this pattern.

3. Close your eyes. Imagine a marble in your mind. Notice the color. What color is it? The color is not significant, but imagining it is. Visualizing the color puts you in your imagination. Imagination opens up the neural pathways. Imagine moving that colored marble–whatever color your imagination desires–down from your brain and plugging it into your

heart. Then, imagine or visualize your heart radiating beams of light like the sun. Fully engage your imagination.

4. Place your fingertips on your sternum and begin tapping or thumping. Your thymus gland resides right behind your sternum. Tapping–like acupuncture–stimulates this energy meridian point, stimulates the thymus gland, and opens up the heart. Notice how it awakens the heart and lungs, and makes you feel stronger. Notice how it stimulates your energy system. Feel it assist in the opening of your heart. These are all good things in preparing for a shift.

5. Now breathe. You're going to take a total of thirteen breaths. The first twelve breaths represent a completed cycle of experience. After the thirteenth inhale, hold your breath as long as you can until you feel like releasing. The thirteenth breath is the doorway to transformation and a new level of consciousness. Breath number thirteen sends you into a gamma brainwave state and recodes the old patterns, birthing something new. For a detailed how-to guide on the breath work, refer back to chapter ten, *YOU ARE THE BREATH: Breathing from Your Heart* (p. 107). Here's a brief summary:

When you inhale, imagine breathing deep into your heart.

Take deep, exaggerated breaths. Fill up completely from the bottom of your lungs all the way to the top. For inhalation through the mouth, pull the air through your teeth so that it's audible. Inhalations through the nose should be robust, meaningful and complete.

With each inhale, imagine the O_2 encoding you with new information, per your intention.

Exaggerate each exhale and push all of the air out of your lungs, expelling it completely. For exhalations through the mouth, allow your lips to form an "o" as if you're saying "ooh" and blow the air out. Exhalations through the nose should be deep, complete and profound.

Imagine releasing and eliminating the pattern you are clearing with each exhale.

Repeat this pattern of deep, exaggerated inhales and exhales for each type of breath in your personal series of breath work, based on your brainwave states.

6. Continue tapping and notice the energy returning to your heart.

Notice how good it feels to reclaim all of the energy you've been giving away to this pattern.

7. Repeat the steps above for the each remaining series of breath exercises if your energy is stuck in multiple brainwave states. Or if you did not measure where your energy is stuck, do all four breath work patterns to cover your bases. The more you do, the higher you get.

RECALIBRATE VIBRATIONS

Once you've completed all of the breath work, go back and see what's changed. Recalibrate each of the following vibrations:

1. Feel into the intensity of each emotion on your heavy emotions list and note the intensity. You will find that most or all of the charge is gone. Things should feel pretty neutral. For the sake of keeping it easy, let's continue to work with our example– frustration, anger, trapped/suffocated have completely dissipated, and sadness has significantly gone down in intensity.

Heavy Emotions	Scale 0–10		Light Emotions
	Start	Finish	
1. frustration	9	0	compassion
2. anger	9	0	relaxation
3. trapped/suffocated	8	0	liberation
4. sad	10	2	happiness

2. Feel into the intensity of the memory associated with the first time you felt the root emotion. Rate it. A lot or all of the charge should have dissolved after the breath work. If you find you still have intense charges, repeat the same series of breath work.

Memory Associated with Emotions:

_____

_____

Starting Intensity   0-10 _____

Ending Intensity   0-10 _____

3. Now, calibrate your ending vibration. You can muscle test or use tipping, or just use your intuition. Say out loud and test, "My ending vibration is at a forty-five." Forty-five is the frequency of love, peace and gratitude. It is a point of neutrality. From this vibration, you can have gratitude for the pattern you are letting go because it helped you to learn and grow. You have gratitude for any suffering because you are turning it into awareness and releasing the pattern.

Ending Vibration: _____

4. Next, calibrate each of the following:

Body Full of Soul %

Self-Love %

Ready for Organic Life Path %

Notice the shift. Notice your numbers before the HEAL Technique® and compare them to the results you achieved after. Each of these measurements should be at or near one hundred percent. Trust that a shift has taken place. Excellent work! Do the happy dance! You will continue to process and shift throughout a few sleep cycles. It doesn't hurt to take some time to meditate, journal and reflect on your HEAL session, either. This helps to integrate the work and your newfound wisdom.

Body full of Soul %: _____/_____

Self-Love %: _____/_____

Ready for Organic Life Path %: _____/_____

Notice the difference. How do you feel? What new insights have you gained?

New Insights:

_____

_____

Congratulations! You've given yourself an amazing gift. What a shift! Give yourself a little gratitude for having the courage to do this work.

As you clear the subconscious patterns that block you from living the fullest expression of yourself, you will become so present in your body and build up so much self-love that you will find you don't get as entangled in the patterns as you used to. You'll become much more aware of those little buggers and empower yourself to bust out of the ones that don't serve you. You'll see a shift in your thoughts and inner dialog, and learn to change belief systems that get you stuck. You will reclaim lost energy that you used to give away to patterns and programs that didn't serve your highest good or your true purpose. You'll catch yourself when you're in your head and quickly redirect yourself back into your heart. *You will be inspired* to love yourself for you who really are so that you can awaken into your grandest vision for your life. Do the work and you will experience true change. As you change, your brain changes, molding you to become the highest expression of your soul.

As you clear these patterns and free stuck energy, all of this becomes possible.

THE HEAL TECHNIQUE® WORKSHEET

Name: _____   Date: _____

What you would like to shift:

_____

_____

Starting Vibration: _____/_____   Ending Vibration: _____

Body full of Soul %: _____/_____

Self-Love %: _____/_____

Ready for Organic Life Path %: _____/_____

Mine: _____

Someone Else: _____

Something Else: _____

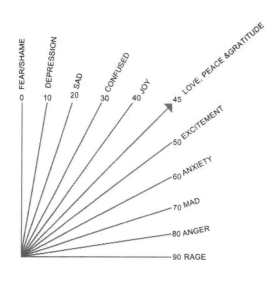

Brainwave States:

1. Beta: _____ 2. Alpha: _____ 3. Theta: _____ 4. Delta: _____

    MM   MN   NN   NM

<u>Crossed Emotions</u>

Heavy Emotions:	Scale 0–10		Light Emotions:
	Start	Finish	
1. _____	___	___	_____
2. _____	___	___	_____
3. _____	___	___	_____
4. _____	___	___	_____
5. _____	___	___	_____
6. _____	___	___	_____
7. _____	___	___	_____
8. _____	___	___	_____
9. _____	___	___	_____
10. _____	___	___	_____

Memory Associated with Emotions:

_____

_____

Starting Intensity 0-10: _____

Ending Intensity 0-10: _____

Begin the HEAL Technique®:

Notice the order of the breath work– work backward from four to one:

4) NM: _____ 3) NN: _____ 2) MN: _____ 1) MM: _____

1. State out loud: *I set the intention to eliminate the pattern in all layers, all levels, and all combinations, without creating a negative response and with unconditional love. I also set the intention to neutralize the memories that ignited this pattern. I set the intention to reclaim all of the energy that's been leaked by this pattern.*

2. Close your eyes. Imagine a marble in your mind. Notice the color. Plug the marble into the center of your heart. Notice your heart radiating beams of light like the sun. Begin to use your fingertips to tap on your sternum. Take full, deep breaths in & out thirteen times. On the thirteenth breath in, hold it as long as you can.

3. Notice the energy returning to your heart. Feels so good, doesn't it!?

4. Repeat steps 2 and 3 for remainder if energy is stuck in multiple brainwave states.

5. Recalibrate vibrations. Notice what has changed. All set? Now do the happy dance!

New Insights:

_____

_____

_____

_____

_____

Additional blank worksheets may be downloaded from healingsimplified.com and healingenergyandlearning.com.

THE HEAL TECHNIQUE® WORKSHEET

Name: _____ **Date:** _____

What you would like to shift:

_____

_____

Starting Vibration: _____/_____   Ending Vibration: _____

Body full of Soul %: _____/_____

Self-Love %: _____/_____

Ready for Organic Life Path %: _____/_____

Mine: _____

Someone Else: _____

Something Else: _____

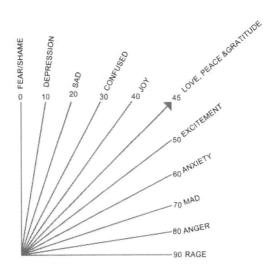

Brainwave States:

1. Beta: _____ 2. Alpha: _____ 3. Theta: _____ 4. Delta: _____

    MM   MN   NN   NM

<u>**Crossed Emotions**</u>

Heavy Emotions:	**Scale 0–10** Start Finish	**Light Emotions:**
1. _____	___ ___	_____
2. _____	___ ___	_____
3. _____	___ ___	_____
4. _____	___ ___	_____
5. _____	___ ___	_____
6. _____	___ ___	_____
7. _____	___ ___	_____
8. _____	___ ___	_____
9. _____	___ ___	_____
10. _____	___ ___	_____

Memory Associated with Emotions:

_____

_____

Starting Intensity 0-10: _____

Ending Intensity 0-10: _____

Begin the HEAL Technique®:

Notice the order of the breath work– work backward from four to one:

4) NM: _____ 3) NN: _____ 2) MN: _____ 1) MM: _____

1. State out loud: *I set the intention to eliminate the pattern in all layers, all levels, and all combinations, without creating a negative response and with unconditional love. I also set the intention to neutralize the memories that ignited this pattern. I set the intention to reclaim all of the energy that's been leaked by this pattern.*

2. Close your eyes. Imagine a marble in your mind. Notice the color. Plug the marble into the center of your heart. Notice your heart radiating beams of light like the sun. Begin to use your fingertips to tap on your sternum. Take full, deep breaths in & out thirteen times. On the thirteenth breath in, hold it as long as you can.

3. Notice the energy returning to your heart. Feels so good, doesn't it!?

4. Repeat steps 2 and 3 for remainder if energy is stuck in multiple brainwave states.

5. Recalibrate vibrations. Notice what has changed. All set? Now do the happy dance!

New Insights:

_____

_____

_____

_____

Additional blank worksheets may be downloaded from healingsimplified.com and healingenergyandlearning.com.

THE HEAL TECHNIQUE® WORKSHEET

Name: _____   **Date:** _____

What you would like to shift:

_____

_____

Starting Vibration: _____/_____   Ending Vibration: _____

Body full of Soul %: _____/_____

Self-Love %: _____/_____

Ready for Organic Life Path %: _____/_____

Mine: _____

Someone Else: _____

Something Else: _____

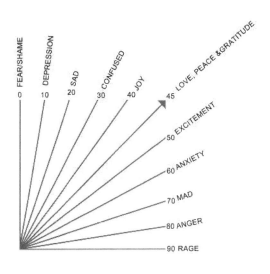

Brainwave States:

1. Beta: _____ 2. Alpha: _____ 3. Theta: _____ 4. Delta: _____

    MM   MN   NN   NM

<u>Crossed Emotions</u>

Heavy Emotions:	Scale 0–10 Start Finish	Light Emotions:
1. _____	___ ___	_____
2. _____	___ ___	_____
3. _____	___ ___	_____
4. _____	___ ___	_____
5. _____	___ ___	_____
6. _____	___ ___	_____
7. _____	___ ___	_____
8. _____	___ ___	_____
9. _____	___ ___	_____
10. _____	___ ___	_____

Memory Associated with Emotions:

_____

_____

Starting Intensity 0-10: _____

Ending Intensity 0-10: _____

Begin the HEAL Technique®:

Notice the order of the breath work– work backward from four to one:

4) NM: _____ 3) NN: _____ 2) MN: _____ 1) MM: _____

1. State out loud: *I set the intention to eliminate the pattern in all layers, all levels, and all combinations, without creating a negative response and with unconditional love. I also set the intention to neutralize the memories that ignited this pattern. I set the intention to reclaim all of the energy that's been leaked by this pattern.*

2. Close your eyes. Imagine a marble in your mind. Notice the color. Plug the marble into the center of your heart. Notice your heart radiating beams of light like the sun. Begin to use your fingertips to tap on your sternum. Take full, deep breaths in & out thirteen times. On the thirteenth breath in, hold it as long as you can.

3. Notice the energy returning to your heart. Feels so good, doesn't it!?

4. Repeat steps 2 and 3 for remainder if energy is stuck in multiple brainwave states.

5. Recalibrate vibrations. Notice what has changed. All set? Now do the happy dance!

New Insights:

_____

_____

_____

_____

Additional blank worksheets may be downloaded from healingsimplified.com and healingenergyandlearning.com.

TESTIMONIALS

At HEAL, we get so many calls and emails after classes, seminars and sessions to update us on how the HEAL Technique® has transformed clients. It's kind of trippy how many of those conversations start out with a client exclaiming, "You're never going to believe what happened!" but we always believe because we're big believers in the power of you. We've witnessed so many healings. We've seen so many miracles. Our clients tell us the most amazing stories. Here are some of them...

I was part owner of a problematic commercial property. We put it up for sale, and three contract sales fell through at the last moment.

I ordered the HEAL Technique®. As I began to use the method, childhood and distant past memories of humiliation and deprivation came to my recollection. After finishing the process, I felt no sorrow or fear about the worst of my childhood memories. A refreshing confidence and high expectations emerged. In less than a week I received the first check for my property, and now I have received $73,000.

It's so exciting using the HEAL Technique® to break through stuck areas of life and relationships. It is an amazingly quick, easy, powerful method to transform any area of life. Overall I feel much more peace, gratitude, wellbeing, and joy.

- Linda Larson, Associate Pastor of Holy Shabach Miracle Center in Lake Worth, FL

The HEAL Technique® is truly amazing. I've had so much personal growth in such a short period of time. For the first time in my life I can say that I am truly happy and at peace.

- Eunice Flanagan

I've been working closely with Carolanne for several months and I love the HEAL Technique®. My life has opened up to possibilities I never imagined possible. Before learning the HEAL Technique®, I was searching for answers on the outside. The HEAL Technique® taught me to look inside for the answers and I have found a treasure chest!! I was able to clear several emotional blockages from my childhood and today I feel great!! WOW!! No one would have guessed deeply repressed emotions could cause such havoc in one's life. I'm so grateful to have such a simple, easy tool.

- Lori

The HEAL Technique® was something I had never experienced before. I knew I needed a change as I was going through a very difficult time in my life, specifically with relationships. I am not someone to go to a regular therapist and just speak about my problems so I did some research and I found Carolanne's healingenergyandlearning.com web site, and her energy instantly captured my attention. I fell in love with her immediately and the HEAL Technique® is amazing. It changed my life in what felt like twenty minutes!! The result of this quick decision was absolutely life changing. Within a few days I felt like an entirely new person. I felt on top of the world and madly in love with life and myself! I had not felt that way before. Even those around me noticed the glow in me! I had been in relationships that constantly broke me down and took away from me. It's as if going through the process of the HEAL Technique® removed all of that negativity and put my missing pieces back together! For that, I will be forever grateful!!

- Meggie Soliman

I have been going to Carolanne for many different reasons for over ten years now– for physical, mental, emotional and spiritual healing. I have literally never once left after a session of doing the HEAL Technique® and not felt incredible. As for physical healing, I had two questionable pap results that required further testing, but each time I arranged to see Carolanne first and went through the HEAL Technique® process in order to change the energy, and when I had more extensive testing done, nothing could be found! The same thing happened after two problematic mammograms. The doctors said they didn't know what had occurred, but everything looked great. I can't even fully explain how the HEAL Technique® works, but I always get results. Carolanne has researched, learned, created, originated and integrated so many different methods of healing that the HEAL Technique® has been able to help with each dilemma I've had. My life is happier, more fulfilled, more peaceful, and I feel even more connected to a higher power because of the time I have spent with Carolanne using the HEAL Technique®.

- Marie Gregory

After forty-five years of study in the healing arts, Carolanne Anselmo stands out as one of my most enlightened teachers. I have had several very important breakthroughs while working with the HEAL Technique® and I highly recommend it to my own clients. It has helped me to melt old wounds so my life is richer, happier and more profound.

- Rev. Ann Emerson, Director of the Sanctuary of Sophia in Lake Mary, FL

Here is a story for you and a thank you... I am currently up in Massachusetts as my partner's mom was very sick and we came up here to be with her before her passing. She passed peacefully in August, but it has been very sad as you can imagine. Now we have no idea when we are coming back. I took this opportunity away from things to give my resignation to my job on Friday which, as you can imagine, was also stressful and difficult to do. I was feeling pretty good physically but after the funeral I started to get really congested. I woke up this morning coughing like a mad person. I thought back to our session when I broke my rib, got a piece of paper and a pen, and did the HEAL Technique® on myself. I realized that I still had in my cellular memory a fear of change and moving. I realized that when I am afraid of a big change, I have an allergy attack and sinus congestion. As I went through the process of the HEAL Technique®, my sinuses suddenly began to drain. I completed the thirteen breaths and really started to feel good.

It was so easy. Just by sitting down with myself and releasing the self-defeating pattern that was occurring, I was able to work through it. Now, forty-five minutes later, my head it not bad at all and I haven't coughed a

bit. I share this for two reasons: First, so you can be reminded of how wonderful the HEAL Technique® is, and second, to remind myself how important it is to remember that I can access this tool and use it to change anything in my life in just minutes. I want to thank you for teaching me this valuable tool. I realize now that I can deal properly with whatever change is occurring... and hopefully return to Florida soon!
- Dru Ann, HEAL Technique® Practitioner

As of this past June, the HEAL Technique® has relieved my digestive issues, restored intelligence to my immune system, the candida I battled with for years is gone, I've strengthened my ligaments to keep my bones in place, expanded my lungs allowing me to take in more oxygen, improved my posture (someone said I looked taller and I noticed I had to adjust the rearview mirror in my car), improved my eyesight, greatly increased my energy (diagnosed with adrenal and chronic fatigue syndrome, plus thyroid disorder and PTSD), gained self-confidence, am having better relationships, removed blockages allowing me to manifest my highest good, greatly improved my outlook on life, and so much more. Using the HEAL Technique® has basically given me my life back! If I knew of this technique years ago, it would have saved me thousands of dollars spent on therapy, pharmaceuticals and unnecessary suffering.
- J. A.

The HEAL Technique® has been hugely instrumental in my work as a physician. Both personally and professionally, the HEAL Technique® has accelerated my growth and helped me to move closer to my explosive potential. In the healthcare field there are often wounded healers struggling along with their patients. Integrating the HEAL Technique® into my practice has helped many complex health problems with incredibly simple solutions. Attending the HEAL Technique® workshops, reading the articles, and experiencing the power of the work has greatly changed my life. Any transformation impacts the whole both globally and universally. I won't miss any opportunity to work with you again in the future!
- Dr. Ramah Wagner, Wagner Chiropractic and HEAL Technique® Practitioner

I cannot begin to express to you the gratitude I have for you and how you have been such a monumental instrument in my life-changing shift into consciousness. You have been a teacher and a mentor to me. I now know I need to and should live in my heart space, and live in my truth!

I was able to overcome many emotional and mental blockages that I didn't even know were there. The HEAL Technique® was able to help me reach within my soul to get to that space to release all that was holding me back from reaching my full potential. Thank you from the depths of my heart and soul for guiding me to reach my truth. I now live in flow with life and embrace what is given to me on a daily basis.
- Kelly Lamoriello

The HEAL Technique® has really changed my life in many ways. My practice has skyrocketed, and I feel I am a more effective healer. I have witnessed profound changes in my clients' lives, and in my life as well. I am so very grateful.
- Isabel, HEAL Technique® Practitioner

When I originally signed up for the HEAL Technique® workshop I wasn't really sure what to expect. I am so glad I attended. Releasing major traumatic memories that have been trapped in my cells was incredibly uplifting, as though I was no longer emotionally affected by the trauma that kept haunting me all my life. It was better than anything I've ever done in my life and I felt like electricity was going up and down throughout my entire body!

After a restful night's sleep, I woke up the next morning and felt a little tired and experienced some flu-like symptoms for a few hours. I didn't have a fever or a headache, but I felt completely exhausted. I later learned that I had experienced a complete purging or detoxification as a result of my workshop experience. When I woke up the day after, I was completely energized and happy! I can honestly say that the workshop gave me confirmation for the first time in my life of who I am, where I'm going, and what my true purpose in life on Earth really is!
- Kamran

I really enjoyed the HEAL Technique® workshop and feel that I have benefited greatly! Since my healing session, I have felt like a new person! When I came home that day, I caught my reflection in the mirror and I had

to stop and look at myself. I could see the change in my eyes! It seemed I had a clear view to my soul, and it looked at peace. I have been facing a lot of challenging things in my life this year. I don't feel the anxiety that I had before the class.
- J. M.

Words are not enough to thank you for sharing the HEAL Technique® with all of us the way you do! You are an incredibly special teacher and healer!
- B. C.

What can I say! If I had met you three years ago, I would have saved about $6000 in counseling, which never worked anyway. After one session going through the HEAL Technique® with you, I have found my happiness. You really know how to spread the love. Thanks again.
- Mike Peterson

I have now made it fourteen months without a shingles outbreak– a new record for me! As you know, shingles outbreaks are triggered by stress. I have been through some extremely long, drawn out, stressful situations this year that in the past would have certainly triggered severe outbreaks, and still have remained outbreak free. I have not taken the daily meds that I used to take, either. I believe working with the HEAL Technique® has truly removed the virus from my body, and that is such a blessing. The HEAL Technique® is a powerful and fascinating force you are working with and I am happy to be fortunate enough to share in this process with you. Thank you so much.
- Sharon M. Thompson

I just came home from my son's school this morning and he was awarded the A/B honor for the third trimester. This is huge for us. This was a little boy who cried not too long ago about how he felt so dumb and stupid because school was so hard for him. His success has to do with hard work and from removing blocks with the HEAL Technique®.
- Anne W.

I just wanted to take a minute to thank you for the awesome healing you have given me in the last week. The HEAL Technique® is an amazing thing and provided exactly the healing I was desperately in need of. A few minutes with you doing the HEAL Technique® achieved results that will stay with me for a lifetime.

- Denise

I've always been fascinated by the power that the subconscious mind silently exerts on each of our daily lives. We all seem to think that the logic of our conscious mind is what determines our beliefs and actions, especially in how we react in stressful situations and interact in our relationships. That is just dead wrong. In reality, so much of what we do is actually determined by belief patterns learned early on or from the most unusual sources that are buried deep below what the conscious mind can perceive.

I can honestly attest that the HEAL Technique® has had a more profound, positive impact on my life than anything else that I have ever experienced. Old belief systems, destructive behavior patterns, fears, worry, etc. are all gone. Looking back, it is clear that I was trying to change my environment so that I would eventually be happy. I had it all backwards. Through the HEAL Technique® sessions, I changed and everything shifted. My life is fundamentally improved. That general, underlying, almost constant sense of unease about the future is just gone. There are times that I experience peace at a level that I never dreamed possible.

Want to know how it works? Certain techniques are employed that allow one to shift one's brainwave frequency so as to move past the conscious mind and blah, blah, blah. The truth is that I really don't have a clue how it works. But who cares? It just does. And it's easy. I like easy. I'm good with easy.

I'm not suggesting that there won't be days when I slip back into old habits, but those wayward behavior patterns don't seem to last, and if they ever do, I can just go back for a tune-up. I have the utmost respect for Carolanne– her HEAL Technique® works. Try it for yourself and commit to more than just one or two sessions so that you can experience the full benefit. All you have to lose are your fears and behavior patterns that have been holding you back.

- Michael Gregory

ACKNOWLEDGEMENTS

Tonya: It is with tremendous gratitude that I acknowledge Carolanne Anselmo, my soul sister, without whom there would be no HEAL Technique®. She–and this amazing little technique–opened me up to a great state of remembering. Remember? The process of coming into my own power has been so deeply gratifying. Carolanne's story became the raw material that allowed me to finally write, a lifelong dream. I am truly grateful to be the conduit for delivering such a profound message.

A huge thanks and a million kisses go to my husband, Paul Turrell, who looked after the kids many, many nights so I could write. Much love and gratitude for my two boys, Tai and Jei. I'm glad we signed a sacred contract to do this mother-son thing in this lifetime. I love you more than mere words can express. I love you with my full heart, all of my soul and my whole being. A big shout out goes to Allison M. Schultz, for her edits and for giving me the momentum to complete this project.

Carolanne: I want to acknowledge my greatest friend and biggest fan, who listened to me spout each wild a-ha, who gave me the space to change my mind a million times and to totally tear his belief systems apart; to my biggest teacher of unconditional love, the love of my life, my husband, Joey Anselmo. I am so grateful that my children selected me as their mommy. Joey and Sunny, you are such blessings in my life. Words cannot express how much I love you both. You "get it," and that's all that matters. I would also like to honor my parents, who gave me a life full of openness and love, and continue to support me as I fulfill my purpose as an instrument of transformation. Thank you to my sister and brother. We are one heck of a tribe. I love you.

A special thank you to Core Love. What a breath you have provided. You're a breathwork genius! To Kaitlyn Keyt: I love you, my ping-ponging geek-out girlfriend. VibesUP is the HEAL Technique® in physical form! To my clients: Each and every one of you is a part of my soul family. My warmest love goes to the sun, Big Daddy-O.

Finally, to Tonya Cox Turrell. When I first met Tonya, I knew she was special. In life, when you find a really good friend, a friend who always has your back and who doesn't judge, you know they'll be in your heart forever. The way that she listened to my out-to-sea stories and put them on paper in a way that everyone can understand is remarkable, but she did it and I have never been so grateful in my life. Without her, I may have never been able to share this with you, this amazing transformative healing process that is about to take place in your life. I love you, soul sister.

FOOTNOTES

i Einstein, Albert. *The World as I See It.* New York: Citadel Press. 2006.

ii Yeager, Chuck. *Yeager: An Autobiography.* New York: Bantam Books. 1985.

3 Luke 17:21.

4 "Oprah and Panache Desai: Change Your Energy, Change Your Life" *Super Soul Sunday.* Season 4, Episode 411. February 24, 2013.

5 Emoto, Masaru. *The Hidden Messages in Water.* Hillsboro, Or.: Beyond Words Pub. 2004.

6 Watson, Lyall. *Lifetide.* London: Hodder & St. 1979.

7 Ibid.

8 Darwin, Charles. *The Origin of Species.* 1859.

9 Darwin, Charles. *The Descent of Man.* 1871.

10 Snooks, Graeme Donald. *The Collapse of Darwinism: Or The Rise of a Realist Theory of Life.* Lanham, Md.: Lexington Books. 2003. P. 57.

11 Loye, David. *Darwin's Lost Theory of Love: A Healing Vision for the 21st Century.* San Jose: toExcel. 2000.

12 Grout, Pam. *God Doesn't Have Bad Hair Days: Ten Spiritual Experiments That Will Create More Abundance, Joy and Love in Your Life.* Philadelphia: Running Press. 2005.

13 Einstein, Albert and Leopold Infeld. *The Evolution of Physics.* Cambridge: Cambridge University Press. 1938.

14 Bell, Rob. *What We Talk About When We Talk About God.* San Francisco: HarperOne. 2013.

15 Taylor, Jill Bolte. *My Stroke of Insight: A Brain Scientist's Personal Journey.* New York: Viking Penguin. 2008.

16 Foundation for Inner Peace. *A Course in Miracles.* Mill Valley, Ca.: Foundation for Inner Peace. 1992.

17 Brian G. Dias and Kerry J. Ressler. "Parental Olfactory Experience Influences Behavior and Neural Structure in Subsequent Generations." *Nature Neuroscience.* Volume 17, number 1. January 2014.

18 WebMD. "RLS." WebMD. <http://www.webmd.com/brain/restless-legs-syndrome/restless-legs-syndrome-rls>.

19 McCraty, Rollin, Mike Atkinson and Dana Tomasino. "Science of the Heart: Exploring the Role of the Heart in Human Performance." HeartMath Research Center, Institute of HeartMath. Publication No. 01-001. Boulder Creek. 2001. P. 4.

20 McCraty, Rollin. "The Energetic Heart: Bioelectromagnetic Interactions Within and Between People." Institute of HeartMath. 2003.

21 McCraty, Rollin, Mike Atkinson, Dana Tomasino, and William A. Tiller. "The Electricity of Touch: Detection and Measurement of Cardiac Energy Exchange Between People." *Brain and Values: Is a Biological Science of Values Possible.* Mahwah, Nj.: Lawrence Erlbaum Associates, Publishers. 1998. P. 359-379.

22 Einstein, Albert. "About education." *Ideas and Opinions.* London: Souvenir Press. 2005.

23 Glass, Bill. *Expect to Win.* Dallas: Bill Glass Ministries. 1998.

24 Lutz, Antoine, Lawrence L. Greischar, Nancy B. Rawlings, Matthieu Ricard, and Richard Davidson. "Long-Term Meditators Self-Induce High-Amplitude Gamma

Synchrony During Mental Practice." Proceedings of the National Academy of Sciences of the United States of America (PNAS). Volume 101, number 6. 2004.

[25] Hay, Louise. *Heal Your Body.* Carlsbad, Ca.: Hay House. 1984.

[26] Hebb, D. O. *The Organization of Behavior.* New York: John Wiley & Sons Inc. 1949.

[27] Skinner, B. F. *Science and Human Behavior.* New York: MacMillan. 1953.

[28] Hanson, Rick. "Mind Changing Brain Changing Mind: The Dharma and Neuroscience." *Insight Journal.* Summer 2009. <http://media.rickhanson.net/files/MindChangingBrain.pdf>.

[29] McCraty, Rollin, Mike Atkinson and Dana Tomasino. "Science of the Heart: Exploring the Role of the Heart in Human Performance." HeartMath Research Center, Institute of HeartMath. Publication No. 01-001. Boulder Creek. 2001. P. 4.

[30] McCraty, Rollin. "Coherence." Institute of HeartMath. <http://www.heartmath.org/free-services/articles-of-the-heart/coherence.html>.

[31] Rosenthal, Joshua. *Integrative Nutrition: Feed Your Hunger for Health and Happiness.* New York: Integrative Nutrition Publishing. 2014. P. 168.

19662807R00110